W9-CEJ-373

STUPID BLACK GIRL

Essays from an American African

By Aisha Redux

With art by Brianna McCarthy

Street Noise Books
Brooklyn, New York

For my parents, the villages that raised me,
and all who held conversations with me along the way.

Street Noise Books
195 Plymouth Street
Brooklyn, NY 11201

Copyright © 2020 by Aisha Redux
Illustrations copyright © 2020 by Street Noise Books

All rights reserved.
No part of this publication may be reproduced or transmitted in
any form or by any means, electronic or mechanical, including
photocopy, recording, or any information storage and retrieval system
now known or to be invented, without permission in writing from the
publisher, except by a reviewer who wishes to quote brief passages
in connection with a print, online, or broadcast review.

Library of Congress CIP data available.

ISBN 978-1-951-49100-0

Illustrated by Brianna McCarthy
Edited by Ashleigh Williams and Joshunda Sanders
Book design by Liz Frances and Charice Silverman

Printed in the United States

9 8 7 6 5 4 3 2 1

First Edition

Table of Contents

Introduction

I wrote this book to heal. Forces greater than myself were pushing me to confront crucial life experiences and to share them with the world in order to process things with clarity and truth. I don't presume to know all the answers, but I do know that the personal breakthroughs that I experienced have led me to great epiphanies and realizations, as well as some intriguing discourse. Ultimately, this all helped me to arrive at a better place.

First, the reader should understand that the American African experience is different from the African American one. It is more than a play on words. I am a first-generation American with West African parents, culture, and heritage, not a descendant of people who were brought to this country in slavery generations ago. There are ways in which these realities overlap, but they are different. And my life is about navigating three worlds. First is the world from which I came. The second one is the world I am now a part of. The third is the world that I want to create for myself. Who am I as a result of all this? Who do I want to be? What am I taking with me into each world and what do I want to leave behind? What about my religious beliefs, or the smell of rice on my clothing on my way to school? Do I feel a sense of pride? Sometimes. The truth is, I feel alien in all three worlds, and I probably always will. But it makes for a unique perspective from my place as a constant outsider looking in.

This book is more than a collection of my narratives. Original artwork by Brianna McCarthy adds a whole new dimension to my work. These beautiful illustrations are Brianna's personal artistic responses to my essays. It is my hope that they provide insight and perspective on the stories I am telling, and that they encourage the reader to pause to reflect and form their own reaction. Growing up in an environment surrounded by a lot of African art heightened my appreciation for where I came from, and originated my strong connection to the visual world. Brianna's art helps bring the writing full circle in a way that is deeply personal. This is my story in the fullest sense.

Above all, I write in hopes of having people feel and connect with spirit in tow. I hope to stimulate some intense dialogue around the topics I cover. My observations and opinions are derived from my own personal experiences that I am sharing with you here. But I want this book to encourage self-discovery. As the reader, you bring your own unique perspective to the table, and I hope you will take this opportunity to share your own stories, to start discussion, and ultimately, to heal.

Origin Story

When I first met you, I thought you were just a Stupid Black Girl.

People often ask me about the title of my platform. Some are intrigued while others are offended. But honestly, I didn't choose this title—the title chose me. The first time I heard the phrase "stupid black girl" directed at me, I was having a deep conversation with an acquaintance. We were in the middle of some philosophical banter, and I was contributing some insightful thought—I was dropping gems on him. I am an only child, so I've spent a lot of time assessing things from a distance. I like to think I'm pretty introspective and analytical. In the midst of our talk, I was opening his mind and expanding his consciousness a bit, so it seems he felt the need to acknowledge that in his own way. But he expressed this through a filter of ignorance and bigotry. Maybe it's relevant, or maybe not, that he happened to be a midwestern white boy. But he said, as if it was some sort of flattery, "When I first met you, I thought you were just a stupid black girl."

This didn't hit me completely right away. He said it so casually that I don't think I even took the time to process it. It flowed out of his mouth with no idea that it might be offensive, like I was somehow already privy to a truth. But the power of this phrase seemed intensified by his casual delivery. It wasn't intended as a vicious jab he hurled at me. We were still there discussing, and he slipped up and let his true colors show, maybe even the true colors of much of society, and that's what lingered with me the most.

When I think back to the time we met, I wasn't acting any more stupid or "black" than anyone present. I was at a party with my friends enjoying myself. But through this filter of his, I was existing in a state of "stupid black girlishness" until proving otherwise. I told a few people about the conversation and about being called a "stupid black girl," and they all responded with shock that anyone would openly say this to my face. A couple of people even said, if it were said to them, they would've responded violently. I understood the reaction, somewhat. But the truth of the matter is, while this guy might have been the first person to say it to my face, he certainly wasn't the first person to deliver this message to me. He certainly wasn't the first to demean or disrespect me like this. You see, this message had been delivered to me before in various ways. Through being undermined, or whitesplained to, or belittled because of my race and gender.

Somewhere deep down, I knew that isolated rage wasn't the answer. It wouldn't even come close to equal retaliation. My rage had to be bigger than that; maybe it could even serve a higher purpose and amplify a message. The message wasn't that I was trying to prove I'm not a stupid black girl. I can do that simply by existing. The message is that I refuse to pay for anyone's ignorance. The message is to make it very clear that there's nothing isolated about this situation. The message is fuck you.

I want to tear down this hierarchy that society has etched into our minds about where a Black woman belongs and cast it away as bullshit. The message is a bold, subversive, and provocative exclamation to say that I'm well aware that society feels threatened by a Black woman's intelligence and power. So threatened that a bigoted insult is offered in the disguise of a backhanded compliment. As an artist I can take certain liberties. And I am taking liberty with this phrase that's been thrown at me by hanging it on a big shiny banner for all to see, sit with, and process.

Through a filter of bigotry, I was expected to be stupid. I am a multilingual person from NYC, who grew up around a lot of intelligent people. I'm thoughtful and I'm a writer. Why was I expected to be stupid? How did the nuances of who I was get seen as stupidity anyway? They didn't. I was simply expected to pay for everyone's ignorance and uphold the order of things. And I'm certainly not here for any of that. I wonder how the full scope of Black womanhood measures up. Do we all just exist on a spectrum between "stupid black girl" and "angry black woman"? Through that lens, probably.

But this phrase prompted an even deeper exploration of myself beyond my race and gender. What did these precise words mean in relation to *me*? Time to self-assess. I wasn't a stupid black girl. But was I a *stupid black girl*? Could this phrase be a moment of reckoning? A girl I was not, I was a woman. But the "stupid" part was something that I wasn't quite sure of. I consider myself intelligent, but I don't necessarily consider myself smart. I always regarded the words "smart" and "stupid" as more of an extension of your actions than your capabilities. "Smart" as being able to make things work for you, and "stupid" as being unable or unwilling to make things work for you.

Stupidity is generally defined as a lack of intelligence and common sense. But there are other ways to interpret it. James F. Welles has a different perspective. In his book *Understanding*

Stupidity, he defines stupidity as "prevention from adapting." He says that stupidity itself can be either innate, assumed, or reactive. And that it can even be a defense against trauma or grief. He distinguishes stupidity from ignorance, explaining that stupidity involves knowingly acting against your own best interests. BINGO! This hit home, and made a lot of sense.

It makes me think of an encounter I had a while back with a guy who had random psychic abilities. This young dude gave me an unsolicited reading at my friend's house. He made some quick, accurate assessments of my life and my family, and how I had been affected by them. And then, he followed it up with one final assessment. "And you're stupid," he said. I was offended at the time, but now I'm able to connect more dots and dismiss my ego for the sake of healing. I realized that there was something to this. Or, at the very least, maybe it was some kind of weird anointing that paved the way for my embrace of the phrase "stupid black girl" and all the things in my life that have come with it.

All of this thinking propelled me to write this book. I had been feeling creatively and emotionally blocked for a while, and the "stupid" was definitely a factor. I had to stop limiting myself. I needed to confront the things in my life that created this block and made me "stupid." I needed to lift the veil and to proceed with more common sense. And I needed to heal from all of the grief and the trauma. For me, this has required fearless confrontation of myself, and fearless confrontation of the filter through which much of society sees me—the sources of "stupid." How is this same stupidity affecting other people? How are individuals in society preventing themselves from adapting, and how are they acting against their own best interest? What about whole cultures? And nations? I challenge us all to step up with fearlessness and confront the sources of "stupid."

SPIRITUALITY

Finding My God

I grew up in an Islamic home. Both my parents were Muslim, but my father was descended from a lineage of Muslim leaders and was very devout. He expected my respect, but he never imposed the five pillars of Islam on me. When I was in elementary school, and the time came for his evening prayer, he expected me to mute the television so that he could pray, but I was allowed to continue watching Nickelodeon silently until he finished. I saw the stability and shield that Islam provided for my father. He prayed five times a day. No exceptions, even towards the end of his life—I watched him recite his prayers under his breath as he lay in bed. His dedication demonstrated to me that there was something of value there.

I learned about the Quran from my father during our many conversations and the stories he'd tell me over the years. I loved the beauty, light, and illumination of his faith. What I didn't love were the ignorant and backwards cultural beliefs that seemed to denigrate Islam. I didn't love how power dynamics and social norms debased much of what I felt the true essence of Islam was.

I know a lot of African kids who were force-fed Islam. It always blew my mind how out of touch some parents were with their kids, and how militant they could be in enforcing their beliefs. Trying to impose their religious restrictions only caused their kids to be much sneakier, their outings laid out like covert ops.

All the parents I knew who used their religion as a weapon did so out of an inherent sense of fear, and seemed to have children who were out of control! These kids, some of whom were my friends and cousins, ran wild and had mastered the art of deception—living double lives. They ran the streets, smoked weed, and generally got into trouble. It seemed like a way to gain their own sense of control while escaping and participating in a mild form of payback. Or, God forbid, worse: they were just being normal teens.

There were extreme interpretations of the faith that I continually questioned. Was there really pork in Crest toothpaste? Everything seemed to be *haram*, forbidden by Islamic law. Recently I started to ask myself, "How much of this actually makes sense to me?" I dared to distinguish elements of the faith itself from the rules of a fearful patriarchy trying to maintain a tighter grip on women. This realization unleashed a flurry of thought and I started to think deeply about religion as a whole;,about how subjective, fanatical, and categorical many people are about their love for or hatred of it. As I started to love and understand myself more as a woman, another veil began to lift. I began to realize my power as a woman, and I wondered why I didn't see that power discussed, explained, or examined in the things I was taught, in the way I was beginning to feel and sense it. It became difficult for me to believe that there weren't powerful and anointed women who were prophets themselves throughout religious history. Where were they? Where were their stories? Something didn't seem right to me.

History shows us the strength and heroism of many women. It's hard for me to imagine that women only existed in spiritual history through saintliness and piety, and some sort of perfected gender paradigm or the Mary/Mary dichotomy—the Madonna or the Whore. Did I have to be one or the other? Where were more of the women who healed and cured and saved? Were these women the witches that people were so afraid of? The wicked witches they tied up, loading up their pockets with rocks, and tossed into a lake, waiting for them to sink if they were not a witch or float if they were?

Were they really to be reviled? Or were they powerful women who connected with nature and challenged what society knew of magic? I found these ideas very frightening at first because I had been conditioned to believe that thoughts like this were blasphemous, crazy, or even evil. I struggled, but I kept pushing forward. I started reading about women's roles in ancient civilizations and made a connection that opened up a new portal for me. One that represented power, defiance, and more importantly, ascension.

In a passage about female menstruation, I read that women were to be feared during this time because of all the power they supposedly possessed. They were described as spiritually stronger and able to manifest their wills—womanifest. During menstruation, a woman often experiences heightened emotions and physical pain, and provides evidence that they have the power to bring forth life itself. Then I thought about what I was taught regarding menstruation in Islam: that menstruating women were dirty. And because they were dirty, women weren't permitted to pray or fast while on their periods. What if this was just an untruth disseminated to control and strip away another facet of our power? What if a menstruating woman was the most powerful thing ever? What if a menstruating, praying woman was only offensive and dirty to a patriarchal male god? This was an 'aha' moment for me and I've never looked back.

This kind of thinking might be considered radical. But once you start examining the world without fear within the constructs of modern society, you may appear radical. The cornerstone of radicalism is aggressive unlearning. What's radical about me talking about things you don't want to think about? And how about the concept of the Devil? Let's unpack that one without fear.

I don't picture the Devil as a red man with horns standing amid a blazing inferno. To me, it's deeper than that—much deeper. The concept of "evil" is only one part, the part we choose to focus on because it takes the pressure off of us. That little red man with horns exists in some form within every single human being on this planet. An amalgam of the darkest parts of you, bred and cultivated through childhood wounds, traumas, fears, anxieties, phobias, delusion, pain, and guilt. These aren't things we choose, but we all do experience them in some way or another, and therefore all of us have or have had that little red man with horns inside of us. He's tucked away, but for the truly brave—this little man is *confronted*. We may not have control over whether such a thing exists inside us. We do, however, have a choice in whether or not we're going to give him life.

I was having a spiritual conversation with a friend over the phone and we were talking about the good and bad aspects of life. I mentioned the word *Satan* as I was explaining a thought I'd had. My friend quickly responded, "I don't like to say that word, I don't want to give any power to that." This is something I've heard other people say and I believe that it comes from fear—the fear of confronting what needs to be faced. In my opinion, if you're afraid of saying "Satan" or "the Devil," you may also have issues that you're afraid to face. So what you are *really* afraid of?

The traditional Rider-Waite-Smith tarot has a pretty interesting depiction of the Devil on its card. It features a giant horned satyr sitting on a wooden throne. A wooden throne—not a grand or opulent throne but a wooden one, which might serve as a reminder that all things obtained through him are a farce and that he is not worthy of being served. Also depicted are male and female demons in bondage; this stands out to me as the most significant trap of the little red man.

What's worse than unwanted bondage? In one interpretation, to be bound is to be overpowered, trapped, and often controlled by something you covet, like money or power. Personally, I attribute "the Devil" to vices that hold someone back, ones that control or block you from your blessings or your higher self—the God in you. This little red man with horns is personalized to each individual. For some it might be drinking, or sex, or gambling, or lying, or anger issues. It can even be attachment to someone or something that is holding us back.

Whether the little red man exists within us or through an attachment to someone else who is toxic or negative, I believe the problem must be recognized and dealt with. Within most of us there lies a little red man with horns that must be conquered. Doing so is difficult, and most of us just ignore it, give into our fears, or accept we may never overcome whatever is holding us hostage. One advantage of faith is that it can offer that glimmer of hope that propels us into taking back control over our lives.

Collectively, all our little red men with horns shape how we see the world around us—but for each of us it is a very personal thing. It's your bridge to cross, but not necessarily your cross to bear. It's calling upon your faith and highest self and love to destroy whatever is holding you back. It's a process of letting go and rising up. It's trusting in your creator as well as the God within you. It's knowing you can be saved.

Our own little red man with horns is where each of us can most authentically find God. Experiencing the bondage, breaking it, and confronting the deepest, darkest parts of yourself is how you find the God in you. That's how I would recommend finding God, Allah, Yahweh, Buddha, however you envision a higher power. Be fearlessly vulnerable and acknowledge your struggles. No matter how deeply rooted, repressed, painful, or tragic, they are all a part of you. Pray to yourself. Look yourself in the eye.

As much as I love writing, facing my past pain and reflecting on it has been a hellish journey—but one that allowed me to break free from the bondage. Writing a lot of these essays felt like purges. Hard to get through but so amazing and purifying when I finally did. But there was no other way around it. To be honest, I think that my writing has been the only authentic way for me to be liberated. Through my own talents and God-given strength, I was able to meet that devil that loomed and eradicate its control. Through this book you will take the journey along with me in many parts and perhaps relate and see some similarities in your own experiences. Maybe you, too, will have some epiphanies and awakenings of your own. Get ready.

A Nightmare on Hoe Avenue

Hoe is the name of the Avenue that runs through the Hunts Point section of the South Bronx. It's where I live, and the vast majority of my nightmares occur here. In addition to my personal juju, this area carries a great deal of its own.

Hunts Point is known for the huge market of the same name, one of the largest food distributors in the world. The area is heavily plagued by crime and poverty and has long been one of the poorest Congressional districts in America. Down the block from the market, there is a sectional area of benches on a street called Amadou Diallo Square, a tribute to the Guinean immigrant who was brutally murdered in the Bronx twenty years ago. Diallo was shot forty-one times by the NYPD in a case of mistaken identity. As a child I remember Diallo's death sending shockwaves through the country, the city, and the small Guinean community in NYC. Seeing the street sign is a reminder of all this. The juju in this area is indeed strong.

I have had issues with night terrors for a huge chunk of my life. When I think back, I remember having problems sleeping even when I was a small child. Very vivid, scary images and emotions came to me at night. I can attribute a large portion of it to anxiety and not really being able to express any of my deep emotions. My parents were never on good terms and spent the majority of my childhood not communicating with each other. This created a tense environment that left a deep, unshakable well of anxiety within me. But it's also given me an uncanny ability to sense hidden moods and emotions in rooms where they aren't being expressed.

A few years ago, my cousin Makeda came for a visit. Makeda is someone whom I always felt very comfortable discussing personal issues with. She, too, had problems sleeping and had been prescribed a sleep aid. We are both West African women and first genera-tion. We grew up with very similar stress factors that were mainly cultural: fighting to integrate our own identities in Western nations with our African backgrounds. We were both also very in tune, in a spiritual and emotional sense, and thor-oughly enjoyed exchanging supernatural interpretations of the world around us. Makeda had been experi-encing a great deal of tur-moil at this time. She was coping with the aftermath of being horribly beaten by her husband and was on medication. This incident was particularly difficult for Makeda because she was well known in the community. She felt a sense of shame for being a victim of domestic violence. A great deal of her identity relies on her tough-girl exterior, and having to experience that level of vulnerability with everyone was especially painful. We both were having continuous nightmares and sleep disturbances and spent a lot of time telling each other about our nightly horror shows.

Last summer was probably the most stressful summer I'd had in years. My financial situation was very shaky and I was breaking away from people and patterns in my life. I was completely uncompromising on the things I would and would not accept; even my tone of voice had changed. I knew intuitively that this was a time that I needed to spend focused solely on me. I had always been a source for people to unload on and unpack their problems. I spent a lot of time worried about my friends and trying to save them, but last summer I didn't have time for it and selfishly considered all that energy as a burden and liability. I didn't want to be anyone's sounding board or anchor, and I didn't much care how anyone felt about that.

But this process was very new to me and it began to weigh heavily; in hindsight, it was like a death. I was letting go and creating an entirely new existence. I had been consciously working very hard over the last couple of years to face my anxieties and traumas, and ground my mind and spirit. I was using plant medicine to aid the process, along with reading books, staying accountable, and not running away from the things that may hurt. In short, I was finally allowing myself to *feel* and experience things I would normally have blocked. I was accepting myself as a whole being as opposed to a partial one. This was scary and was manifesting in many ways, especially in my dream state.

Makeda had arrived from overseas for a vacation and was staying with me for a couple of days. The first night of her visit, I woke up screaming. I was having a nightmare where I was being chased by a dark shadowy figure. This is something that hadn't happened to me in quite some time. But this last summer was an exception to everything. My stress levels were so high that I didn't menstruate at all that summer, and my moods were completely uncontrollable. Sometimes, I would have intense crying sessions alone. I was suddenly processing my feelings and my past. I was talking to my dead father, I was breaking shit, having breakdowns, telling my mom about things she had done that had fucked me up—feelings that I hadn't even been conscious of until I was screaming about them at the top of my lungs. It was all just pouring out. It was painful, but it also felt good. I was proud of myself for finally allowing myself to purge, and to feel.

The next morning, I brought up my nightmare to Makeda. There was no way she missed the display because she was sleeping right next to me. Her reaction was kind of bizarre. She looked nervous and didn't have much to say, except, "Damn, you still go through that? I thought all that was over with. I don't have that problem anymore."

I thought her response was callous and it left me feeling more alone and even weirder than usual. She continued to explain how practicing her faith and devotion to Islam was why she was nightmare-free. I couldn't believe that she was taking advantage of my moment of vulnerability to spew some sanctimonious, holier-than-thou bullshit. I felt like a "batshit crazy heathen" subjecting my pious friend to a Freddy Krueger revival during her holiday. I also began to realize how different we were from each other. I was delving straight into my issues and finding solutions that were real to me. I am close with Makeda. But we resolve to heal in very different ways. In my eyes, she hadn't actually fixed or treated anything. She was just retreating to repression. But that's on her. Makeda represents a part of me and where I come from that I had to leave behind. The comfort of having all the answers presented to me wasn't working for me.

I was ready for all the nightmares and whatever else it took. That summer ended and my period finally arrived. That shadowy figure appeared once more after that in a dream, and with it came some new consciousness and courage. This was making me stronger. I was finally ready to turn my sorrow into force. My nightmares began navigating me to safety. There was some new juju on Hoe Avenue.

Yage

Your perspective on life comes from the cage you were held captive in.
—Shannon L. Alder

Plant medicine is a pervasive theme in my life story. If I made my life into a film, it would play a supporting role. As a child however, I didn't quite get it. My mother always had an assortment of tonics in her bedroom closet and drawers. She would have remedies made of herbs, sticks, and leaves sent from Africa. The arrival and opening of the packaging was always quite exciting!

My mother's theory was that using the tonics consistently over long periods of time would allow them to seep into you. They were an aura and quality-of-life investment. After enough consistency and usage, the fruits of all your labor and ritualized devotion would be rewarded with a beautiful and coveted inner alignment. There would be a glorious explosion within you, your light would burst through, and—Alas!—a magnetic force field.

When I was young, I assumed all of this was figurative, not literal. It made me think of the mid-eighties martial arts cult classic *The Last Dragon*. In the movie, the main character, Leroy Green, reaches the final stage and is able to concentrate mystical energy into his hands and cause what is called "The Glow." Only a true martial arts master would be able to attain "The Glow" over his entire body. This concept applies outside of martial arts and the movies. I believe that releasing the glow is a result of tapping into your greatest self and grabbing the essence of your being. Self-realization creates a physical glow and an impenetrable force field manifests around you. The process is less dramatic than the film, but it is definitely a real thing.

According to my mother, this process comes in part from sacred plants. I didn't start thinking deeply about sacred plants until just a few years ago. I started by exploring ideas like the benefits of drinking lots of water, and how eating fruits and vegetables could impact your system to become a lifestyle on its own. My mother's principles of natural human alignment could be viewed as a pyramid. And this would be its foundational tier. Another tier would consist of implementing supplements, herbs, and alternative methods of healing yourself in order to become stronger. Another tier would include adding natural substances that had transcendent and spiritual properties. Things that would work on levels deeper than just the physical but go to the soul, to the emotions and the mind. These effects could create life-altering results that would shape a new framework for an entire belief system in itself.

My mother has always been in the habit of sending me

packages filled with natural healing substances. Last fall, she sent me a batch of herbs and dried leaves from a forest in Mali to brew and bathe in for three days. She said after the first day I would feel weightlessness. She was right—it felt like a baptism! I've never felt that level of cleanliness and lightness before. I felt like a newborn, with a renewed sense of urgency to find freedom from some deep-rooted things. I wanted my spirit to match the weightlessness I was feeling physically. I knew I needed to put more effort into rooting out things that might be holding me back in life. I needed to unblock feelings of past trauma, depression, and grief. The potential of it felt fucking powerful. I wanted to go deeper. Perhaps there was another tier? Things that my mother hadn't dabbled in and had no knowledge of. Plants and beliefs that weren't rooted in Africa, but in other parts of the world. Plants that would take you on a journey. Plants that were considered drugs by the majority of the Western world.

One day I stumbled across a TV episode of journalist Lisa Ling's CNN series "This is Life" that explored Ayahuasca. Ayahuasca is a thick brown substance used in spiritual rituals indigenous to Amazonia. I became so intensely curious that I read about its effects on those who drank it, effects like extreme nausea and hallucinations. And I was fascinated by claims likening one Ayahuasca ceremony to ten years of therapy.

The active component in the brew is DMT, a chemical substance that occurs in many plants and animals that can be consumed as a psychedelic drug and has historically been prepared by various cultures for ritual purposes to induce a spiritual experience through an altered state of consciousness. I couldn't let it go and was tempted to try Ayahuasca for myself. I did a good deal of research by talking to a lot of people who'd tried it and experienced its effects. I actually put an ad on Craigslist to find people who had done Ayahuasca and would be willing to talk to me about it. Some people told stories about feeling utterly terrified, and some said they'd been so changed they'd devoted their entire life to the practice of ingesting the plant. The one thing most of them had in common was the impression of dying. Was I really ready to die, or to even imagine dying? I have to admit, that scared me. The idea of hallucinating my own death seemed too intense; then I wondered whether the "death" people were experiencing was possibly more of a death and re-birth of their spiritual selves.

I truly believe my lifelong spiritual studies, along with my being open to new experiences, allowed me to have this experience. After all, this was not something I wanted to try out of mere curiosity. I wholeheartedly believe in spiritual cleansing and had a very specific intention for participating in the rituals. My intention was to let go of the past that might be blocking me. To be able to move more fearlessly through life. To turn my pain into power. I followed all the guidelines suggested and even fasted for a couple of days before the ceremony.

From the very start, I understood Ayahuasca would not solve all my problems or remove all memories of past traumas. First and foremost, a person will resolve nothing if there's no belief in the power Ayahuasca holds. Without it, the ingestion of Ayahuasca is nothing more than taking a drug in search of a high or trip. One's intentions must be firmly in place before even thinking about partaking. Lacking focus, Ayahuasca is eas-ily misused or abused, so it can in turn abuse you, manifesting itself negatively as a bad trip.

I researched for an entire year and became certain that this was a spiritual experience I was destined to have. Pushing any lingering fear aside, I decided to attend an Ayahuasca ritual myself. A friend of mine put me in touch with a shaman, who sent me an email invite to a ceremony being held at a dance studio in Brooklyn on a Saturday evening. When I arrived, there were about twenty people there. I was the only Black person. I didn't feel connected to anyone there, and it seemed very strange. I didn't understand why these white people were here, because I never connected this level of spirituality to whiteness. Some of them looked like super models to me. I started to wonder if this was really just a trendy thing. I wanted to delve deep into my problems, and I worried that this wasn't going to be what I was looking for.

Everyone was instructed to wear comfortable clothes, to bring their own yoga mats, comfy blankets, pillows, and a water bottle. We set ourselves up on our yoga mats around the sides of the room. The shaman came in. He didn't look like your stereotypical shaman. He wasn't wearing flowing robes. He didn't have a long ponytail. He looked more like a college professor, wearing a tweed jacket and glasses. He stood in front of us and started telling us his story. He was from Peru and had a thick accent. He had been studying plant medicine and Ayahuasca for twenty years. There was an intellectual quality about him that made me more comfortable. He called us up one by one to drink a small cup of the thick brown bitter-tasting liquid. And we went back to sit on our mats.

I sat there waiting, and within twenty minutes I experienced the "death" people described. I believe each person's "death" occurs at different times along that individual's spiritual path. One person's "death and rebirth" may happen in a day or a week. Others might experience that "death" as a transitional phase, taking months or years for their life to change significantly. I suddenly found myself on my back, not knowing how I'd gotten there, arms together and eyes closed. It was. . . peaceful. Warmth poured into and through my body, and when it stopped, a window into my soul opened and I began a journey I'll never forget.

I learned a lot about myself in that session. It allowed me

to see things I was unsure of that were holding me back. Any remaining fears vanished, and I allowed sensation to take over. And I learned about others as well. Initially I hadn't felt connected to the other people in the room, but watching them experiencing things alongside me helped me see their vulnerability. Everyone was completely disarmed. There was no way around it. We were all there because we needed to heal. And that was what connected us. I didn't vomit during the session, but I cried. And when I was saying goodbye, the shaman told me that I needed to be more in touch with my emotions. This was something I knew, but hearing him verbalize it was a turning point for me. As the effects wore off, I realized I'd been irrevocably changed. I walked out of that room feeling worn but revitalized. Light. Like a drenched towel wrung completely dry.

During their transitional period, which begins with the ceremony but continues long after, people's lives are changed. Their blinders are removed, and they make painful discoveries about themselves. Some have to hit rock bottom before they can change their lives, and a single ceremony may not change anyone's life. A single experience may simply be grasping the key to the door of transition. It might take several, or even many, experiences before a person can truly open that door to change. Partaking in an Ayahuasca ritual only signifies a readiness, a preparing for that "you" to die. Like ending a relationship, you have to be ready to face what comes after.

I looked at death and the concept of it differently after that. I thought about the title of the Biggie album *Ready To Die* and saw the meaning of it differently—being ready to die meant being prepared to accept harsh truths and feeling ready to move on.

What if this transitional period was really a means of understanding and accepting physical death? There are many ways people die. Spiritually or physically, it is my belief all are reborn in one way or another. After this experience, I believe when this earthly body dies, we are reborn with greater consciousness into another realm where we begin the process again. You fulfill your mission here and then you are ready to die. Everyone's time is different. Some lives last an hour and others a hundred years. It depends upon the path chosen.

Through my first Ayahuasca experience, I gained a new outlook and understanding of the complexities of death and the varying ways we experience it throughout our lives. I became braver and less hesitant to meet the necessary obstacles I had to overcome. Accepting the death of things, and knowing there is a transition to bear, made me stronger and blessed me with a greater, more beautiful perspective of life.

The second time I did Ayahuasca, I focused on something else entirely: my Black consciousness and the dissolution of a patriarchal influence from my God consciousness, scraped fucking clean. Because I knew that Ayahuasca heightened one's spiritual awareness, I thought it might be interesting to incorporate something that could boost my experience. I live in the South Bronx where there are botanicas, shops selling spiritual objects and alternative medicine products, nearly everywhere. As a person who believes in the power of such things, I often frequent the one around my way. A couple months earlier, I picked up a scented cologne called "Cologne of Oshun." Oshun is an orisha, one of the Seven African Powers in an ancient and powerful traditional African spiritual path known as Ifa. A number of religions, such as Santería in the Caribbean, are derived from Ifa, which assigns deities or emissaries like Oshun authority over different aspects of nature and life processes. When I first discovered the Seven African Powers, I found it freeing. It was a way of seeing God that factored in my blackness.

Oshun intrigued me in particular. For me, seeing a Black woman as a manifestation of God was life-altering and I was definitely all in. Beyoncé introduced much of the mainstream world to Oshun in her visual work for her album *Lemonade*. But Oshun has been around for thousands of years and is rooted in ancient belief.

Oshun is the goddess of rivers and streams, fertility and beauty. Her color is yellow, and her flower is the sunflower. Her personality is not what one might imagine for a traditional deity. She isn't saintly. She isn't reserved or humble. Oshun does her own thing!

I grew up in a home with a lot of Black art. My father was an African antique art dealer. He collected it and was a connoisseur. I vividly remember his magazine clippings of beautiful Black women all around the house. The groundwork for my spiritual understanding was laid out from childhood, which was crucial in a society that doesn't exactly go out of its way to uplift the image of the Black woman. Our beauty and intelligence is often undermined and disrespected, and we are frequently reduced to the lowest form in representation. It was great to have a spiritual entity whose purpose debunked that, reinforced us, and was detached from all the Eurocentric and colonial trimmings and trappings.

So I doused myself with the cologne of Oshun and went in for my second Ayahuasca ceremony. It was held at the same place in Brooklyn with the same shaman. But my hallucination was completely different this time. It wasn't just visions and intuitive directions; it was guided by a rather snarky and very direct female energy and voice. She was making observations about the surroundings, she was exceedingly confident, and she wanted me to throw everything away and just focus on the message that God was a Black woman! She kept repeating it over and over and over again.

She was forcefully pushing me towards a deeper integration and inner understanding. I felt like a child being thrown into the deep end and being instructed to swim or die. It challenged my entire concept of what being a powerful and ascended Black woman meant. If this narrator was any indication of what divine female blackness entailed, it certainly flipped the table on everything I imagined. She wasn't silent, sage, and glowing. She was snide, confident, and uncompromising. This gave me a lot to process after the ceremony. I thought about Black women that I knew or who were in the limelight who might resonate with this powerful voice.

I didn't tell anyone about this particular ceremony. My self-awareness told me that repeating this aloud sounded "crazy." I personally didn't think it was crazy, but I didn't want to share what I regarded as a pivotal, necessary, and sacred experience with people—only for them to degrade it. I was stepping into some very new and uncharted territories. Engaging in Ayahuasca rituals still carries a lot of stigma. I just wanted to think for myself, find my own power, and connect my own goddamn dots.

Whatever this all meant, I knew it represented what the Ayahuasca experience wanted me to learn that day about the world and myself. This is what Ayahuasca thought I needed—the affirmation of a Black female God in my consciousness. A shameless acceptance of a creator that's reflective of me. This was me turning my back on a society that is shaped by whiteness at the expense of everyone else. Things that were forged and warped within me by society, I had to undo through hallucinations and a Peruvian shaman.

I also understood that there might be someone sitting across from me at the ceremony who had a similar hallucination, narrated by the voice of a completely different deity. What they were getting was what they needed to get, what would heal them and make them into their best selves. I believe the concept of God is simple, yet so vast that it cannot be neatly placed in a single box. Just as there are an immense number of perspectives on life, there exist many attitudes and beliefs about God. God is intrinsically different to everyone, yet seems to govern the universe equally. You can ask one hundred different people "How would you describe the world?" and get one hundred different answers. No two people experience things the same way, even if their explanations are similar. The hand you are dealt in this life, your experiences, and your reactions to them, all determine how your life unfolds. Each person exists in their own reality. I, along with anyone else in that room, was seeing God as it was—an internal projection.

My third Ayahuasca trip, a year later, but with the same shaman in that same dance studio in Brooklyn, was a life review. It was the most logistical experience of the three. It felt like my brain had been snatched out of my head, thrown in a washing machine, and placed back with instructions of how to proceed. If you know anything about me, then you know that an instructional life review is something I could greatly benefit from. It was like an entire checklist of trauma that I went through in order from least affecting to most. One of my major issues was coping with my father's death. It had been a few years, but it was still very hard for me to process that I would never see him again. It was particularly hard for me to grasp that we would never have any more conversations, and that he wouldn't be able to relay his wisdom to me. The thing that came to my mind and spirit during that part of the journey was lentils. My father loved cooking lentil soup. This was a connection and way of still holding on to him. Whenever I missed him, I could still share a meal with him by having lentil soup. It would also be a way that I could keep him around.

Ayahuasca is now something I consider part of my "spiritual diet"—different karmic food groups that come together to provide nourishment for your soul. It is your duty to explore and find which best suits you. Although I have a strong spiritual base, I have still been affected by the millennial shift into spiritual individualism and am seeking my own answers. DMT is one of my answers.

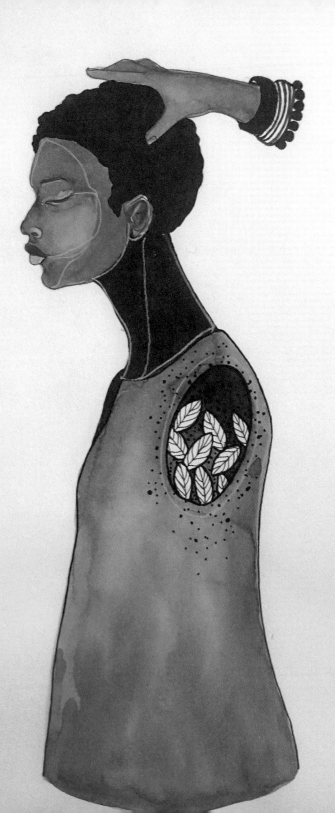

Djibril's Story

Ten years ago, my cousin Djibril had a mental breakdown and ended up surviving the scariest ordeal of his life. Witnessing his harrowing journey opened my eyes to one of the great contradictions of the modern world. Seeing how mental health is treated in the West versus how it is understood through a more spiritual lens, I was struck by how a society that has so much can still know so little. This modern society that is advanced and evolving scientifically seems astoundingly ignorant of the potential power of what nature has to offer. Djibril's harrowing psychological and spiritual odyssey greatly impacted my consciousness and belief system. His is an example of people struggling with mental and spiritual health in the Black community within the context of the Western world.

As a child of African immigrants born and raised in Paris, Djibril grew up in one of the suburbs, *les banlieues Parisiennes,* raised with a blend of Western ideology and hard-core traditional African practices. Djibril's father is Catholic and his mother is Muslim. Djibril converted to Islam when a wave of fundamentalism was overtaking the French ghettos. Until 1958, Guinea was a French colony, so a lot of Francophone Africans immigrated to France and settled in these suburbs, which are deemed unsafe or subpar; they are where much of the minority immigrant population is forced to reside.

Djibril was a slim, jovial young man with skin the color of dark mahogany. A couple of years prior to his breakdown, when Djibril was about 18, he grew a beard and stopped listening to secular music. He gave up his beloved hip-hop for his belief in Islam. I witnessed this conversion when I visited Paris for the summer. Djibril was living with my aunt, his sister, and another cousin of mine in an apartment in Garges–lès–Gonesse.

With his beard and long garb, his demeanor reminded me more of our great uncles and respected elders, not that of a teenager. There was something very different about Djibril. He was moving closer to Wahhabism, a puritanical and ultra conservative practice of Islam, which was sweeping through the neighborhood. His sister rather bluntly said that he had been brainwashed. The majority of Muslims denounce Wahhabism and think of it as more of a sect. It's extremely strict and from my experience, members tend to be either very quiet around others or very verbal and disdainful. They consider themselves the "real" Muslims. I must preface again—this practice of Islam is not practiced and recognized by the majority of Muslims and these are the Muslims that are more closely associated with extremists and jihadists.

At the time, racist hiring practices in the French job market were also affecting Djibril. Once he finished school his mother, my aunt Binta, grew concerned with his continuing unemployment despite having successful and promising interviews. Djibril had been diligent about seeking employment in Paris, but the prospects were slim. A young black man from les banlieues was not anyone's top pick. So Aunt Binta called in a favor with a cousin of hers who worked at a middle school. Djibril was hired to maintain order in the school and supervise the students. This middle school, however, lacked any real discipline.

The students seemed to be the ones calling the shots. As the only boy in a household that adhered to strict patriarchal norms, Djibril was both spoiled and sheltered by his parents, and thus ill-equipped to navigate struggles like this one. Djibril wasn't able to control the chaotic environment—he lost his bearings and often describes his experience there as traumatic.

Djibril's faith helped him cope. One evening on his way to the Mosque after work, Djibril met a fellow Muslim brother named Rashid, a vendor who gave him a plaque on which a surah was inscribed. He told Djibril that it would protect him from spirits like the djinn. Muslims believe the djinn to be spiritual entities that are created from fire. They exist in an alternate realm, so we cannot see them—but they see us. He took the plaque home and immediately started feeling strange. That evening, his family came home and discovered Djibril semiconscious. Djibril didn't mention anything about the plaque.

The next day, Djibril went to see Rashid to get some answers. When he arrived, Rashid wasn't there, and he was greeted by another man. While Djibril was explaining how the plaque had affected him, Rashid arrived. The man admonished Rashid, "Do not give something like this to someone without warning them of its power." He told him that when played through a recording, the surah is powerful enough to invite negative spirits. But Djibril didn't know any of this, so he had incorporated it into his evening prayers. The man offered to do a ruqya on Djibril, a chanting of divine words to cast out evil djinn. In other words, he wanted to perform an exorcism. By then, Djibril didn't trust either of the men, so he declined and left.

Day by day, over the next few months, Djibril's overall mental state and physical condition rapidly degenerated. He started having intense hallucinations and nightmares. He described feeling trapped in chaos: sinister voices commanding him to do dangerous things, even to kill. He saw beings floating around him, and he lost the sense of time passing at all, one day taking a shower and staying there the whole day. Out of desperation, he decided to see a spiritualist who was recommended to him to find out exactly why this was happening. This man gave Djibril a bath meant to cleanse him, body and spirit.

But the bath seemed to make Djibril's sleep state worse and intensified the hallucinations. He began to feel more and more like he was being pursued by something very dangerous. His mother decided to go with him to the mosque to speak to the imam in order to gain perspective and perhaps get a thorough spiritual interpretation of the situation. Upon meeting with the imam and the people of the mosque, they concluded that there was nothing wrong with Djibril. "Perhaps it is a fabrication of the mind," they said. That assessment wasn't helpful because Djibril's situation remained the same.

Djibril seemed to sink into a mental abyss as things got worse. He described it to me this way: "I felt paranoid, like everyone wanted to harm me." Since the approach of the Muslim community in Paris didn't seem to be working, there was only one solution that Djibril's family thought feasible—send him to Africa where there was a whole world of alternative treatments to be found.

Many West African families living in Western nations send their children back to get saved or cured. Growing up, unruly kids were warned we might be sent back to Africa, with the implied assumption that a child who was acting out had forgotten their roots and grown too comfortable in Western society. It never seemed to occur to anyone that a child's behavioral problems might be due to emotional or psychological issues such as Djibril's. But in this case, Djibril's journey to Africa was meant as deliverance, not punishment.

It was a month-long trip, but it felt much longer to Djibril because things got worse. He went from one spiritualist, shaman, and witch doctor to the next. The treatments and the baths he was prescribed had a very harsh effect on him both physically and emotionally. There was no sense of tenderness towards him. The focus was on ridding Djibril of his demons, not on actually healing him. Instead, he was being neglected emotionally. Djibril was mentally exhausted and at the end of his rope. He finally visited a clairvoyant who told him he would, in fact, be cured by a woman living in a "high storied building." In the end, Djibril and his family considered the trip to Africa a failure, and when he arrived home, he was placed in a psychiatric hospital.

A couple of weeks later while running errands, Djibril's sister Charlotte ran into his good friend Sofiane, who hadn't seen Djibril around and asked how he was doing. Charlotte recounted the entire story and Sofiane immediately offered help. His mother, Fanta, was a practicing shaman and made her living helping people with spiritual afflictions via a two-week process. During those two weeks, she gave her patients tea leaves to be brewed and imbibed three times a day and also to be bathed in, as well as incense to burn. Used in conjunction, these treatments would cleanse him of evil.

While Djibril was in the hospital, Fanta visited and gave him teas to drink, administered the rituals, and had him rub a prepared tonic all over his body. She did this continuously for weeks and things finally started to improve. Soon, Djibril appeared normal again and was released from the hospital, but inside he was still being tormented. He went to stay with Fanta's family and was always very serious about taking his treatments exactly the way she prescribed. This all took place in Fanta's home, a "high storied building" in Paris, where she lived with her husband and adolescent children. Her patients were integrated into the family while they were being treated. They all ate together. The patients weren't treated differently because they were sick. I experienced this loving atmosphere myself a couple of years later when I visited Fanta in her home. She generally charged her patients around $400, but she was flexible and was willing to work with people. She had a separate tiny room, "a cave" in the basement of her building filled with African objects where she did her spiritual readings. The room had a palpable, almost ominous energy.

Djibril made it a point never to miss burning the incense or anything else Fanta advised. He even told me about one encounter when he fell asleep without drinking the brew and was abruptly awakened by something urging him to go use it. Within a few months, my cousin seemed to recover completely.

I was astonished, to say the least, when hearing Djibril's story, but I shouldn't have been. Alternative remedies didn't really start becoming popular in America until the seventies, but traditional remedies have been around for thousands of years. They have survived for a reason—they work. In places like Africa, what is considered alternative in Western countries might sometimes be closer to the norm. Especially when we are speaking of non-physical ailments, mental or psychological afflictions.

To me, this wasn't just my sick cousin who was treated and cured through plant medicine—this was a manifestation of something much bigger. I'm not a doctor and I'm not a shaman, but I have a rare and nuanced perspective as a westernized first-generation American with indigenous African heritage. This makes the world bigger to me and adds far more dimension to Djibril's case in my eyes.

George Packer, a writer at *The New Yorker*, described the dynamic between Paris and the suburbs as "schizophrenic" and goes on to say there are "two parallel worlds" in his 2015 article "The Other France." This truly shapes the scope of Djibril's story. Djibril's schizophrenia was mirroring the schizophrenic constructs of the French system. A duality. An opposition. A dichotomy. Djibril vs. Paris. Djibril vs. his mind. Djibril vs. spirits. Djibril vs. society.

When there is no enemy within, the enemies outside cannot harm you.
                                                              —African proverb

I cannot speak for all Africans or say that Africans don't believe in psychology because that would be false. But it seems to me that in West Africa, there is a lack of understanding of how circumstances and behaviors affect mental health. In many ways, this is the inverse of the disconnect between the Westernized world and nature. As beautiful, sacred, and vital as African spiritual belief and culture are, the practice seems to exist in opposition to crucial reasoning and scientific understanding. Plant medicine may have saved Djibril, but it didn't explain why he had been suffering. Fanta's explanation was that Djibril was being pursued by two evil spirits and that she would travel in his dreams as part of the treatment while he was in her home hospital. Although I grew up with a lot of knowledge of mysticism and have heard many stories throughout the years, the Westerner in me thought that entering people's dreams sounded like some wild shit. And where did everything else fit in?

When Djibril had his breakdown, the primary explanation I heard was "Djibril has a djinn problem," which I interpreted as Djibril being haunted. The typical solution among West Africans was to treat the symptom while completely ignoring the root cause. It is my belief that a lack of collective accountability is what ultimately contributed to the existence of these djinn. The community was avoiding responsibility for these man-made monsters. Not acknowledging trauma and repressing it can warp that pain into a demon to be feared and blamed.

This seems common and seems to be what was really making some people sick. Not facing a society's deepest and darkest ills gives way to vicious cycles. In the case of Djibril: a mama's boy from the ghetto was lured into Islamic fundamentalism during unstable times after struggling with unemployment. After he finally gained employment, he was confronted with a challenging environment filled with delinquency and trauma. Wasn't this enough for anyone to snap? Why was I the only one able to see this? This was not just missed by his family, but the doctors at the psych facility too. Were they unable to see the potential stress and trauma that racial, religious, and political oppression could have on a young black man from the ghetto? Or perhaps it was just easier to ignore it.

In my experience, Islam and Christianity seem to look down on the practice of traditional African mysticism and spirituality. The tricky thing is that nature and knowledge of sacred plants and remedies for deep spiritual afflictions are right there at our disposal. There exists a hybrid of Islam and traditional African spirituality that dates way back to the Mali Empire. You are likely to see Islam blended with culturally indigenous practices like plant medicine baths, shamans, and cowry shell readings. It's the actual culture and identity. This is the spiritual blend that I believe most Islamic West African women practice, while the majority of West African Islamic men shun spiritual aspects of their culture. I'm fascinated by the spiritual components and practices of West African culture, mainly because of its authenticity and depth, but also due to how misunderstood it is by the Western world. It's often reduced to evil and scary magic. Why is understanding nature to a greater degree and being able to incorporate it into your life considered frightening? It's only magic to those who don't understand that nature is here for all of us as a transformative gift from the universe, something many Africans understand well. The plants that saved

Djibril are dried leaves that could be purchased in the market-place in Africa for less than twenty bucks. Did this shaman perform magic, or did she just set her intentions on saving Djibril, utilizing her knowledge of nature and all its compounds? What might be perceived as "magic" is often just nature. And what is nature? Nature is God. Besides, I think big pharma is arguably way scarier than these demonic entities could ever be.

What would have happened to my cousin if he had stayed at the psychiatric facility, taken the prescribed drugs, if Charlotte hadn't bumped into Sofiane? Where would Djibril be? Isn't he better off now? Could this form of treatment help other people with Djibril's diagnosis of schizophrenia? Are these spirits in fact a manifestation of trauma? These were just a few things I began to ask myself. What stood out to me were the very distinct ways that Djibril's condition was being interpreted, and the two opposing views of his symptoms from the perspectives of Western science or traditional African medicine. Is it possible that much of what is needed to treat health conditions is available in nature and we just don't know enough about it? What if these two forms of treatment were equally respected and patients were treated by both concurrently?

The point I'm trying to make isn't that everyone who has a loved one suffering from mental illness should seek out a shaman. The idea of containing a spirit through the consumption of brews and burning incense for the rest of your life may not be to your liking. At the same time, the thought of having to control a mental illness by taking a myriad of prescription drugs, whose side effects may be as harmful as the disorder itself, may be just as distasteful. From my perspective, what we define as mental illness can also be seen as a spiritual problem. I don't believe, however, that a shaman is the only way to treat a spiritual problem. I realize that this may open up various different theories, but I want to help begin a dialogue. These two approaches to medicine are based on two fundamentally different perceptions of life. In most cases, the medical doctor in the psychiatric facility couldn't fathom the shaman's diagnosis any more than the shaman could fathom the doctor's. Neither one may be able to see the whole situation, given that both are firm believers that their way is the only and optimal treatment for the problem. But there may be a more comprehensive solution.

What if we concentrated more on how these treatment options overlap and interact with each other, rather than trying to disprove any of them? Perhaps we would find a magical medium. This is the challenging part, because it requires true curiosity and open-mindedness. It's easy to pick a side and argue its merit because you can find evidence—cases that support an idea because of documented successes. It's easy when someone else has done all the work.

But what if you are like me? What if you've been exposed to a variety of cultural value systems, and treatment has multiple meanings? This is the starting point for expanding your consciousness. Instead of just being perplexed and giving up, one can try to search for connections. That's how we begin to evolve, and this is the direction in which we should go. Without an open mind, you're not even in the game.

I don't believe that everything is in conflict. I believe that synchronicity plays a greater part in the universe than we even know. I believe that the universe is perfect in its design, and that we should explore as much of what we don't know as we possibly can. I believe curiosity and flexibility are the best means of change. And that a change is coming.

Enemies

I got enemies, got a lotta enemies
Got a lotta people tryna
drain me of my energy
They tryna take the wave
from a nigga
Fuckin' with the kid and
pray for ya nigga
—Drake "Energy"

Enemies are a pervasive factor in American African awareness and life. It's not that I've felt under siege my whole life, but the times that I have been have felt extremely intense. Being West African, the feeling of being on guard against other people comes with the territory. Naturally, the juxtaposition of wealth and poverty in societies with vast socioeconomic disparity

leads to envy and resentment, and to turmoil. And in some African communities, this can manifest in contentious attitudes that create enemies. From what I grew up seeing and hearing, I consider West Africa to be a truly mystically evolved land but with a very real downside to all the spiritual awareness and wisdom: the practice of black magic and spiritual warfare. This is something that I don't often see discussed and seems taboo to even speak of—especially to non-Africans. But it's certainly a part of the overall African culture, whether people choose to believe in it or not! Some people have the privilege of not having to believe in it. They can just laugh and call it silly superstition. It's not in their world and therefore it doesn't exist.

My mother has always been very frank with me about this since I was a child. She told me we have enemies and people who don't like to see us prosper. I believe this is one of the prime reasons she was so devoted to plant medicine and staying prayed up. Protection and being protected is something that is heavily instilled within me. All my prayers throughout my life have been centered around being protected. My mother believes that these practices have kept us safe from karmic and spiritual attacks sent out by enemies. We might not have known specifically who these enemies were, but their existence was not questioned.

Growing up, I would hear a lot of stories of how old-school African dictators and leaders would acquire power from dark magic and blood sacrifices to dark entities. My mother told me that when she was a child, parents would hide their children during elections so they wouldn't get kidnapped by agents of candidates and offered up to demons in exchange for power. There were countless stories of African immigrants who left Africa, obtained visas, and were prospering in their respective Western nations, only to find themselves mysteriously afflicted with extreme physical ailments or their life suddenly falling apart, prompting them to return to Africa. This was all believed to be secret work from witch doctors commissioned by jealous relatives still in Africa who were vying for their downfall. Just recently, my uncle told me that in Dakar he witnessed droves of people walking around unaware of exactly how the fuck they ended up back in Africa. Why they quit their jobs or left everything behind. In Nigeria, which is perhaps one of the most notorious countries for voodoo and black magic, there is an actual law that prohibits causing or seeking supernatural evil or destruction unto someone.

This never made me paranoid, but it made me hyperaware of people around me and their actions. My way of dealing with enemies, whether they are supernaturally inclined or just haters, is to stay the fuck away. Even on a mundane level, I don't even tolerate basic "frenemies." If you're around me and I sense that intentions aren't crystal clear or you're seeking to compete with me, degrade me, or cause me any shame, I disengage from your life. No explanations. If I notice a pattern of jealousy with people in my life, that's enough for me as well. If my simple existence is enough to throw us both off, then we shouldn't be around each other.

As a child, enemies were introduced to me through bedtime stories. Really scary ones that dealt with supernatural and mystical horror. My mother often told me tales about witch doctors who cursed people who displayed too much hubris. It wasn't until I became an adult that I realized none of that shit was appropriate to tell a small child, and that it probably did more harm than good to my developing mind. Bedtime stories shouldn't be meant to scare you. But my parents were committed to toughening me up and making me aware of the horrors of the world, our world. There were enemies. Upon reflection, I would say that what it really did was create more fear and distance between myself and " the Africans," as I often find myself unconsciously calling these members of my own community. The truth is, part of me considers the African experience as a scary one. Oddly, it feels like this fear made me into a more objective person. I am able to move through things that might shock or frighten others with more swiftness, because my fairy tales were different.

I am no longer walking around in fear of these enemies, and I don't think anyone should. But the precaution that was instilled within me helped ease me into understanding the darker side of humanity. I am not afraid of the truth and of seeing things as they are. At this point, the only enemies I truly fear are the parts of myself left unhealed or unconquered. With very little exception, the majority of bad juju that may come my way is derived from that. I have also learned that there is nothing more powerful and effective than turning a former enemy into an ally. As a whole, we can work on doing that by not only confronting ourselves, but confronting issues within the community that we may be afraid of.

Victor

*This thing of darkness
I acknowledge mine.*
—William Shakespeare,
The Tempest

When I started experiencing sleep paralysis in my mid-teens, it was incessant, terrifying, and unlike anything I had ever experienced. It felt like a presence would enter my room, hover over me, and shut my body down. I didn't know how to make it go away. I didn't make a connection until years later that it might have been due to stress, trauma, and my unhealthy way of ignoring and compartmentalizing my emotions in a blatant disregard for my mental health. But somewhere along the way I decided to call this spirit Victor. I don't know where this name came from, but I stuck with it.

As far as I was concerned, Victor wasn't only responsible for night terrors. I started blaming him for everything. I blamed

Victor for my misfortunes. I blamed Victor for my impulsivity and relationship drama. I blamed Victor every time I felt depressed. I blamed Victor whenever I lost my temper. I blamed Victor for self-destructive patterns and my lack of control. I blamed Victor for not being where I wanted to be in life.

Every time I met someone named Victor, I would freak out. I needed Victor to leave me alone. I began to think the only way to conquer Victor was through being more pious. I just needed more God; I needed more light to cast out this dark figure that had attached itself to me. I told a friend of mine, a born-again Christian, about my dilemma, and she said I should discuss this with some priests she knew. My friend arranged to have two priests come to her apartment in West Harlem to talk to me. The priests told me I needed to convert to Catholicism. I wasn't surprised to hear this. I have an affinity for Catholicism and even factor some of it into my spiritual amalgam, but I wasn't behind the idea of a full conversion to an organized religion. I preferred to collect my data and hold on to what made sense and felt enriching to me. I believed that there were many sources for truth at my disposal; I just had to find them. When I did, I would know. The priests said Victor had entered my life because of my African spiritual beliefs, and that I needed to leave this all behind. As they were talking, I was listening, but I was confused. I thought, but I *am* African. How could any beliefs associated with who I am culturally be considered wrong? As much respect as I had for these holy men, I just wasn't with it.

However, my friend who referred me to the Catholic priests said something that stuck with me: "I don't think that spirit's name is Victor. I think it's taunting you. Victor means winner. That spirit is just asserting dominance over you and wants you to know that he is victorious over you." That gave me a lot to think about. Was I at war? And losing?

About a year later, I met Adam at my friend's house. An

all-American, blond, blue-eyed, tortured kind of guy. Although we seemed like opposites, we clicked instantly. We talked on the phone for hours the next day, with ease as if we had known each other forever. Adam lived on the Lower East Side. He seemed super intelligent and enlightened. He shared a lot of things with me about his personal life: He was an alcoholic and had gone to rehab. His alcoholism had destroyed his family and they cut him off. They told him they would only reenter his life if he decided he was ready for rehab, then they would send him to a facility in Thailand. Adam's life was in shambles. People didn't seem to respect him; he was borderline homeless, and his chi was all fucked up. But one thing was certain—he seemed wise. He told me about a trip he took to South America in which he stayed in the jungle. During an amazing DMT experience, Adam was told by a shaman that he was a healer. I believed that he definitely had a lot of greatness to him but also many issues to work through. At that point I had heard about Ayahuasca, but I hadn't tried it yet and was very interested. I told Adam about my night terrors and anxiety, my self-destructive patterns, my pain, sadness, and confusion. He told me that he knew someone who could help. This man was a Peruvian shaman who traveled frequently to NYC, where he would hold secret Ayahuasca ceremonies in Brooklyn. Adam said he would give me his email. I trusted his judgment—until Adam uttered, "His name is Victor."

This placed me in quite a strange predicament. I thought this was another one of Victor's tricks. I would go to the ceremony, hallucinate, and be trapped in a living nightmare. Or I would go and face a very real fear and find my way to freedom. Instinctively, I knew that I had to get over my Victor fear in order to access Ayahuasca in the most convenient way possible. It was either this route or go to Peru. I was torn. It took me about nine months to get the courage to attend the first ceremony, but it turned out to be a breakthrough for me and helped change my life. Victor the shaman wasn't scary at all. He was a professional and was well-versed in plant medicine.

Things began to change in my life, and soon Victor the spirit was making less frequent visits. I started going to therapy last summer, and one of the things that I needed to unpack with the therapist was Victor. I needed a fresh understanding of Victor that was completely separate from anything I knew or thought or was told. I told my therapist my story, and as she listened, I was hearing myself talk and thinking about how fucking creepy all this shit sounded. I hated talking about things that were this dark and strange because nobody really understood. I told my therapist about a dream I had recently in which a dark figure appeared: Victor. I was frightened in the dream, and the fear overtook my whole body. It was a very physical, active fear. In the dream, the dark figure reached under his face as if he wanted to remove a mask, and it was as if my fear surpassed everything and forced me to wake. My therapist responded, "It sounds like what Carl Jung talks about with the shadow self."

I went home and started doing some research per my therapist's response. According to Jung, the shadow self is a part of every human being that represents the darkest aspects of who they are. It's the hidden part that stores pain, trauma, guilt and vices. It's a part that must be confronted, accepted, and integrated in order to be whole. Jung talked in depth about how religion works to suppress the shadow, like locking a beast in a closet. The shadow cannot go away and its repression can manifest in some damaging and underhanded ways. It will seep through regardless and become even more problematic. He talked about religion being harmful in this aspect, and how some religious people unleash the repressed shadow by projecting it in the form of harsh judgment of those who don't fit their constructs of piety. I certainly had seen and heard a lot of this judgment growing up.

There was one last thing I read that tied it all together for me. Jung talked about dreams and the journey to integration. He talked about seeing the shadow self in a dream and it removing its mask only to find out that it is you. This was the exact dream I had. This is what was being described. I was *floored*. How did Carl Jung know about my very odd dream? If it was being described like this, it meant other people experienced this too. Maybe all of this was normal, in a way? Maybe I was normal, in a way? I felt liberated, and a lot of things started to make sense.

I had always been fighting so hard to get rid of Victor, when Victor was me. Instead of dealing with the things that were burdensome I would pass them on to Victor, in effect never processing anything or accepting myself. After this revelation, I stopped referring to it as Victor and started calling it my shadow self. I began to understand those layers of myself more through doing shadow work: facing my anxieties, confronting issues in my past, and gauging my triggers to find the root of them. I realize now that this thing I hated so much is an essential part of who I am. It's what propels me forward. I wouldn't even be able to sit and write these essays without Victor.

But the most vital lesson I learned was understanding how beautiful and perfect the universe is by design. The value of self-acceptance and transparency. All that is needed to turn your own Victor into a victor.

Tower Terrors

Recently I came across the list of symptoms for Post-Traumatic Stress Disorder (PTSD) when I was doing some research on night terrors. For some reason, I think I assumed the symptoms were always intense and connected to war. But through research, I discovered the symptoms can be subtle, and some actually sounded familiar to me. I may have never been to war, but I did witness the event that called America to the War on Terror.

I was late getting to school the morning of September 11, 2001. I was fifteen, a sophomore in high school. I lived uptown in Harlem and went to school downtown, a couple blocks away from the Twin Towers.

I usually met one of my schoolmates, Natalie, at the subway station on 125th Street and we would commute to school together. On that day, we had a fairly normal journey until we reached Chambers Street station. When we got off the train, a man ran along the platform frantically shouting, "There's a bomb in the World Trade Center!"

Natalie and I decided to exit the station anyway, unaware of what was going on. When we finally emerged from the stairwell, we saw that the North Tower was on fire! We still had no idea what was going on, so I insisted that we continue on to school.

Bad idea. The road we took was on the block adjacent to the Towers. I looked to my right and saw figures falling from the building. It wasn't until I heard the bodies hit the ground that I realized those were human beings leaping to their deaths.

I was shocked and numb, but Natalie started crying hysterically. We were standing on the same block as the Century 21 building when I heard the sound of a plane flying a lot lower than it should. I knew right away where it was headed, so I stared at the sidewalk, refusing to look. It went right into the South Tower.

That's when all hell broke loose. I was sure we were all going to die, but my survival instinct kicked in. I did all I could to remain calm while Natalie started screaming for her daddy. It looked like Armageddon. People were running around crazy and I was in a daze. I couldn't believe I was in the midst of this. It just didn't seem like the type of scene, if witnessed in a movie, that anyone could escape from alive. There was a smokiness.

Nobody knew what to do except run and bug out. We wanted to call someone, but there was no cell phone service and the pay phone lines were too long. Natalie and I walked for miles along with the rest of the Manhattanites trying to escape. It felt like we were walking forever.

Suddenly, it happened—the South Tower collapsed first, followed quickly by the North Tower, and Natalie screamed her lungs out each time. An enormous piece of our adolescent memories were destroyed with them. Hours later, we finally made it to an upper west side station where we took the C train home.

All the businesses and schools in that area suffered tremendously. One thing that made dealing with the aftermath even harder was the imbalanced news coverage after the attacks. One disturbing *Teen People* article had me thinking about a whole set of implications that I really didn't want to deal with at the time. The school that was getting a lot of media coverage was one of the city's specialized high schools, and the majority of the students were white. White privilege still came into play with tragedy like this? This was a school with high profile students, including the child of one of our city's mayors. It had prestige. And it was half a mile down from Ground Zero.

What I didn't understand was why they didn't reach out to the two schools that were literally across the street. The students who were closer to the Twin Towers, and could definitely give more precise and well-rounded narratives, weren't even contacted. Fuck that! Our school was *right there.* The specialized high school reopened less than a month after 9/11. At our school, students were displaced for an entire semester, because the area had to be sorted through. Our school's lobby was being used to store dead bodies. Our school's principal lost her sister in the Towers. Our school, where two of the students had an eyewitness account from across the street. Coincidentally, the school with a majority of Black and Latino kids. Perhaps we were not quite the image of sorrow and devastation they felt would sell enough magazine copies. This was one of my very first rude awakenings to how things worked.

A new era of night terrors began that night after the attacks. I had never experienced anything like it. I remember lying there and feeling a presence swing open the door, approach my bed, and hover over me while I lay there unable to move. This petrified me and became a regular occurrence over the next several years. Yet I still thought I was fine.

I always thought I was fine, but I didn't *feel* fine. My mom asked me one day if I thought I should talk to someone, perhaps a therapist. That's when I really should have known that I wasn't doing a very good job of pretending everything was okay. Never before had I heard my mom mention therapy, let alone suggest therapy or seeing a psychologist. As deeply cultural West Africans, it wasn't considered an option. I was so surprised, but I still told my mom that I was fine.

Writing this with a newly formed consciousness and understanding about mental health and emotional repression, I can honestly tell you that I am still *not* fine. I get anxious when people talk about September 11th. It is very difficult for me when people go on and on, telling their stories about where they were when they heard the news. I relive being across the street while people leapt to their deaths, and I think about all the people who died that day. I think about my principal and her sister, and how we students were displaced while bodies—some dismembered—were stored at my school.

Every time I think about the World Trade Center Mall and commuting every morning with people who worked in the Towers—some of whom likely died that day—I become extremely anxious. When I think about the pain and chaos those people experienced and those suited figures leaping to their deaths, I am overwhelmed and am almost immediately brought to tears. I have yet to visit the memorial—it's still too soon.

But I'm making an effort to stop numbing myself at will and to allow my emotions to flow. I'm giving myself the time and permission to feel all my emotions and cry whenever necessary . . . like when writing this.

SEXUALITY

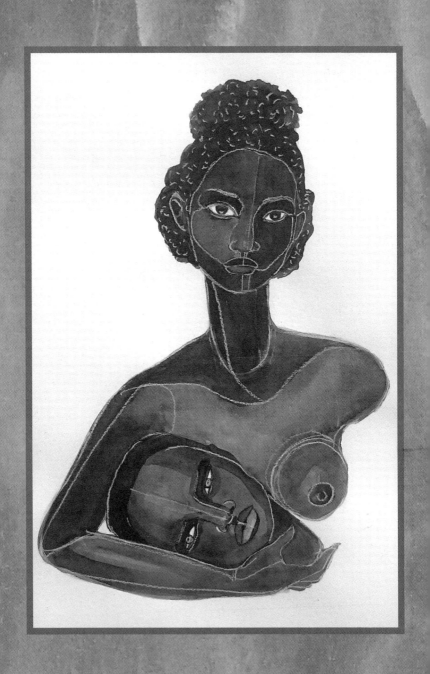

Floating Black Adonis

My man is smooth like Barry,
and his voice got bass
A body like Arnold
with a Denzel face
—Salt-N-Pepa ("Whatta Man")

In 1993, legendary female rap trio Salt-N-Pepa released their monster single "Whatta Man" from their album *Very Necessary*. It was a Billboard Top Ten hit and garnered a Grammy nomination. I was old enough to remember singing along to the chorus and being taken by the awesome display of soulfulness, positivity, and Black girl magic in the video that came along with it. The song is about the idealized notion of Black male singularity and the love of a good Black man.

Girls like me were slowly being seduced by this fantasy of the Black male dreamboat. As I got older, I developed a name for this idealized character: the "Floating Black Adonis." He was the embodiment of perfection. He was handsome and loved his momma. He was street-smart as well as book smart, spiritual and centered, well-endowed and upwardly mobile, and of course, Black and masculine. This wasn't just the standard; it was the target. This man would appear on your way to the top; you would get married, bathe in Black love, and have a bunch of Black love babies. This was the uncompromising goal and it honestly seemed simple enough to me—after all, there seemed to be loads of Black men around.

My reality growing up was that I knew a lot of Black men who seemed to fit this paradigm: intelligent, handsome, educated, employed, and very religious. What I didn't really see were the happy and enduring marriages that I expected as a result. Some women in my family found love outside of our race with partners who assimilated into our West African culture, so the idea of ending up with a white man didn't seem odd to me at the time. But, however appealing this fantasy might be, it is separate from the reality of relationship dynamics between Black men and Black women. From my perspective, there seems to be a disproportionate number of thriving single Black women to the size of the pool of Black men they desire. From the Black male incarceration rate to misogynoir to Black women seeming to advance professionally in this country at rates much higher than Black men, there is quite a lot to unpack. Black women have been upwardly mobile, becoming highly educated and forming businesses and enterprises of their own. The one thing that's always been quite clear to me was the unrelenting quest by straight Black women for this Adonis.

This is something that I discuss with my homegirls. Does this floating Black Adonis even want to be found? But most of my homegirls seemed more narrow-minded and slightly impractical. When I brought this up to a friend of mine, she listened but didn't seem to hear me. Her type was her type. I asked her if she would consider someone outside of her race, and she replied, "No, not really." When I asked if she would consider a sexually fluid man she replied, "Hell no," without a thought or consideration. To my mind, the problem was that the Adonis she was in search of, on top of being highly desirable, was more than likely open to dating outside of his race, and probably open to sexually fluid women! This is what I was noticing from not only what was being portrayed in the media, but a lot of Black men I saw in the city. They just seemed a lot more open to possibilities. These are the men she wanted.

When I was in high school, I remember a particularly funny conversation that I had with my friend where she told us she had heard that white guys turn bright red during sex. I was repulsed by this thought. With all the transformations that already occur during sex—the body heat, noises, and perspiration—I didn't need to look up and see a tomato face caught up in the rapture. To be honest, the image of this rapturous tomato man developed into a latent fear of mine. Eventually, I found out that this was just a silly myth that had kept me from exploring some pretty interesting prospects. And it made me wonder what kind of myths were being spread about Black women. But on second thought, maybe I didn't want to know.

I was curious about sexual fluidity in Black men, a topic that is often considered taboo. The majority of women that I have spoken to about it have responded negatively. There is a spectrum of sexuality, and it follows that Black men are included in this too. Although some bisexual Black men might feel the need to keep the fluidity on the down low.

The floating component of floating Black Adonis refers to him as an unreal figure, but it also applies to the fact that he isn't particularly grounded. He levitates, because he is looking to elevate and move up in life. He might use whatever, or whomever, he needs to in order to lighten the load of his existence and to succeed. This is not necessarily negative, but it's not necessarily positive either.

His good looks garner him the attention of all types of women, which is the primary reason I don't covet the Adonis. Adonis doesn't have a problem dating for clout and social acceptance. This is the major discrepancy between the Adonis and the throngs of Black women that are after him. He might not even be interested. In big cities, this Adonis might not even be open to dating a Black woman, someone who isn't white or mixed race. It is clearer to me that the Adonis is not on the same page as most of the women that want him.

The floating Black Adonis seems to be changing in many ways since "Whatta Man." It's time to question our paradigms. This concept, this figure must be cast aside while we examine our whole history and narrative in relation to his. The unwavering truth is, although he may be the prize, he should never be the rib . . . or the backbone for that matter. The Adonis might lighten his load, and float onwards and upwards from a grounded state and without those vital parts; that's okay. We should just never allow ourselves to lose sight of what we are worth in power as creatures to covet as well.

Come Get This Yoni

Yoni is a Sanskrit word that means "the womb." To me, it also represents the power and strength that emanates from womanhood. Before I knew anything biological or spiritual about my reproductive organs, I felt that it was a universe of its own. A Yoniverse that not only had to be protected, but respected and understood. I had a vagina, therefore I had it all. It's the physical source of my greatest strength and power. Before anything, I was a woman, and to me that mattered. I had to be respected.

It's a tough deal when you've grown into a woman whose Achilles heel is behavior associated with things that are accepted as the norm. Especially when you're outspoken, with a penchant for getting combative and lashing out against the bullshit. This was my deal. Although I am part of a society that normalizes sexism, I had a strong mother and am connected to a subculture that is largely matriarchal. My mother ran things in her family.

Growing up, the majority of African women I knew in the U.S. were separated from their husbands and had to create their own security and identities in this new Western world. I saw the strength and capabilities of women, and that always seemed limitless. I believe this is why it has always been impossible for me to accept mistreatment and disrespect of my womanhood.

When I was an adolescent, I lived mostly in Harlem with my mother. We frequently had relatives living with us. One year, my uncle Kadir, my mother's younger brother, came to live with us. Often more of the family would come by: cousins from overseas, children of my mother's childhood, and family friends who wanted the NYC summer experience. This group was mostly girls. The apartment was spacious, across the street from Morningside Park and just a couple blocks from the Apollo Theater. This was pre-gentrified Harlem at its finest. Uncle Kadir had a very domineering personality. He liked to impose irrational curfews on us, enforce rules, and instruct us when to come home. He was difficult and a pain in the ass overall. My mother, who was the one actually providing for us, didn't seem to have a problem with us enjoying our summer and coming home late. But everything about my uncle screamed old-school and antiquated chauvinism. He never seemed to ask for anything; instead, he would make demands.

My mother always served him a big heap of food on his plate, for all three meals. Food that she cooked. Watching every meal not only cooked for him, but also served and cleared for him, bugged the shit out of me. As I got older, it was something that I began silently protesting. I don't understand how a grown man can't go and reheat his own leftovers and sit down and feed himself. So many men command control and respect from women, yet they are incapable of taking care of themselves without them. In my uncle's case, all the power was false, and the authoritative shit was just a mechanism of control. In my mind, nobody owes you shit for being born with a dick. I certainly don't.

Regardless of what I think now, this dynamic is something that my mother grew up with and that I always thought was

normal as a kid. Uncle Kadir represented to me a very extreme and negative version of the patriarchal system, even down to his gait. It was very macho, borderline comical. It was something out of *Cobra* or some other eighties action movie: The walk of a man stepping into a seedy dive bar about to serve some vigilante justice. The kind of walk that made you want to scream, "Calm the fuck down!" even when he wasn't saying anything.

I remember being the one that would argue with him the most after coming home late. One summer, his daughter, who lived in France, visited with another one of my cousins and two sisters whose parents were close family friends. We were all around the same age. I didn't care much for the two sisters and found them snobby. They had grown up in Ivory Coast with a very bourgeois lifestyle. The older one always complained about how she hated America and only came here for shopping. She didn't understand things like doing her own laundry and would complain about it. I was always made to feel responsible for all of them having a good time, and it felt oppressive to me.

One night, things got worse. The younger of the two sisters, Rumi, came and told us that Uncle Kadir had instructed her to come to his bedroom after everyone was asleep. Just to be extra clear, nothing about this was normal. We were all underage and my uncle was well into his thirties. This was confusing, but at the same time I had an idea of what was going on. Rumi was the most physically developed of all of us. She had breasts and curves, which gave her more of a mature look bizarrely offset with her infantile habit of still sucking her thumb. Rumi's admission surprised us, but I never once thought she was lying. After Rumi brought this up to us, it was never really spoken about again and was completely swept under the rug.

Enraged, I confronted my uncle about it the next day. He claimed that it was all a misunderstanding and that Rumi misunderstood what he said. I knew he was lying. I stopped speaking to him after that and he no longer existed to me.

Although my uncle was a pain in the ass, I usually got along with him and considered this an act of betrayal. I took it very personally. It was pedophilia, threatening and disrespectful to our girlhood, not to mention hypocritical as fuck. Here he was acting as a protector, enforcing these rules, when really, he didn't care at all.

His daughter was kept in the dark about the whole thing and I spared her the story. Uncle Kadir moved away a couple years later and started his own family, so I didn't have to see or hear from him much. To this day, explosive fights erupt between us whenever we meet, and he's still very much a chauvinist.

Coming into my adolescence in Harlem, I had to learn that the traditional rules of respect that I had been taught weren't valued by most boys. My yoni was all bullshit to them. There were rowdy teenage boys on the block who were working out their own immaturities and traumas on the girls around them. They would inappropriately grab and hug on me and my friends and wouldn't always stop when I told them to. I never felt like I was in danger, but it always bothered me to know that saying "NO" or "STOP" to someone the first time wasn't enough. It disgusted me that these disrespectful boys saw girls as objects they could cop a feel off of and laugh.

I made it a point to keep my distance. It wasn't until much later that I learned the stats. According to RAINN, females ages sixteen to nineteen are four times more likely than the general population to be victims of rape, attempted rape, or sexual assault. I wouldn't classify any of this as sexual assault, but I do consider myself lucky. I was never alone with any of these boys.

As an adult, I have come to hear shocking accounts of friends of mine who were raped as teenagers. None of them reported it. As far as I understood, there were things that we were told and there was the reality. We were told that we were girls and had to remain feminine, delicate, and in need of protection. The reality was, we had to protect ourselves and no matter how feminine we appeared, we had to be strong. We had to be prepared for a world that was ready to fuck with us, treat us like objects with no agency, and run off laughing ... or worse. I wasn't here for any of it.

A few years ago, I was looking for a roommate. I needed someone who wouldn't clash with my very traditional, conservative Muslim family that was always visiting. There was a spare bedroom and my mom would come from overseas and stay for months at a time. That means my roommate couldn't drink, do drugs, or be loud or "promiscuous."

I personally didn't care how anyone else lived as long as they didn't steal, were clean, and paid the rent on time. But my family was very different. So the easiest thing was to just find another African who at least knew how to play the double life game. One that would easily snap into character when necessary and wouldn't feel annoyed or upset about it because they understood how shit worked.

I went on Craigslist and found someone who seemed perfect. Oumar was West African too, from Senegal. He was a Muslim, a non-drinker, and he went to Columbia University, where he was seeking an advanced degree. He had a family in Africa, and this was his first time in America. He had just arrived from Senegal a few days earlier and his friend had found me on Craigslist.

His interview went well, and he moved in the following week. Oumar was very quiet and very observant. He was well-mannered and generally presented himself as saintly, pious, and eloquent. His slim build and quiet nature made him seem mild, but I felt there was a lot brimming beneath the surface. My instinct was telling me that I needed to keep things as cordial as possible to avoid trouble. But all that went down the drain when my mother came to visit.

My mother's personality is big. She loves new people, cooking, entertaining, and building lasting friendships and bonds—damn near right away. She liked my new roommate a lot and respected the fact that he seemed focused and religious. She had long conversations with him, cooked some more, and even invited his wife over in Africa to visit the States. I told my mother to ease up. He might be African too, but we didn't know him. I needed boundaries.

Things started to get unsettling for me the day I caught Oumar looking at me from the corner of his eye. My family was sitting in the living room watching TV and I was in the hallway when I saw him very sneakily staring at me while still facing the screen. This might seem trivial, but it's always the small things that eventually give way to bigger clues.

After that came his random antagonisms. He would initiate conversation, ask me direct questions about my life and future plans, only to dismiss them all with snide, disparaging remarks. Like Oumar, I am an observant person and I can see people's games a mile away. I didn't give in. I've had people try this type of shit with me all my life. It's a passive aggressive means of intimidation and control. He wanted to put me in my place, and I could see it. I felt that this dynamic shift could have been avoided had the initial boundaries I set not been crossed by my mother. Otherwise, Oumar wouldn't have felt comfortable enough to bring up things with me that I hadn't brought up with him. The next incident came a couple months later. One evening, I asked him if he could move from the big couch in the living room to the lounge chair because I wanted to sprawl out on the couch. I was on my period and I just wanted to sink into my blankets and watch TV. His response was dramatic: he slammed his textbook and stormed off into his room.

I thought it was strange. I hadn't been rude or forceful. It was a simple request, and this wasn't his fucking apartment in the first place. He was renting a room. Me asking him to sit on the lounge chair wasn't asking for a fight, but it seemed that he was looking for one. I confronted him about it later that night. He told me that it was extremely disrespectful of me to ask him to move from the couch, and that if I wanted to lie down then I should do it in my room. It turned into an argument. Nobody was going to tell me that I couldn't lie down on my own goddamn couch and watch TV in the living room on my period. Fuck that!

But as I became outraged, I was also taking the bait because he wanted a rise from me, and he got one. The next day we had a very heated argument in which I threw a chair across the room and threatened to break his laptop. We stopped speaking. He always remained very calm but would go out of his way to provoke tension, by doing small things like turning on unnecessary house lights or complaining about the noise. All of which would escalate into arguments. One day it came to a head. The cops came. In fact, the cops came again three more times.

To his disappointment, his attempts to get the best of me or control me failed. He might have been used to this tactic back home and perhaps thought that I would feel intimidated, but he picked the wrong fucking person. I grew up in NYC, not Africa. I wasn't going to respect anyone who didn't respect me back. I wasn't afraid of any man, and I also discovered that I had a violent temper and wasn't afraid to show it. This notion of African men feeling entitled enough to act like your husbands or fathers because they were in your space was not going down! It was a mentality that I wouldn't tolerate, and Oumar discovered that the hard way.

I had run out of options and I didn't know what to do. I needed Oumar out because this was affecting my peace of mind.

To feel this way in your own home is one of the worst feelings imaginable. One of my uncles suggested that I file a rape report against him so that he would get arrested and have to leave. As extreme and unethical as that idea was, I actually thought about it for a second but never truly considered it.

A couple months passed, and the tense atmosphere between us started to get to him. He had lost the good graces of my mother, so it was also very awkward for him when my family came to visit. Oumar finally decided to move out, but not before sending a letter to the landlords telling them that I had been illegally renting the room out to him! His final jab. This repressed, conservative man had sought to overpower me in my own apartment. I pitied him. My family speculated this was part of a plan he had to turn me into a docile creature so he could then marry me and get his American papers. That's exactly what two of his friends had done. But I had more power and strength than he expected, and I fought back.

Whether it was in my home or in the world at large, the grids are shifting. From where I stand, I see a tug-of-war taking place between the antiquated patriarchy and the natural progression of women claiming their place in the universe. The patriarchy is losing! This yoni bites the fuck back, bruh, so proceed with caution.

Sex Narrative

I grew up in a Muslim household. In my culture, no one talked about sex, not even in passing. Everything I ever learned about sex I learned from TV, friends, books, or by trial and error.

My mother always made sex seem like a scheme—something boys want and will take from you. When I was a teen, my mom would always say, "Don't give yourself to these boys." That was her way of warning me not to get tricked.

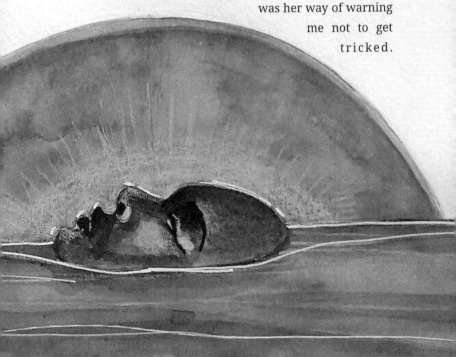

Sex was never treated as an experience that was shared or enjoyed. She made it seem like something boys might snatch away from you if you weren't careful . . . like your wallet. I liked a lot of boys during my teens, but they didn't necessarily like me back. My mom didn't have much to worry about in terms of boys stealing sex from me and running off with it. My lukewarm desirability pretty much kept me safe.

My first real relationship and sexual experience occurred when I was nineteen years old. It was with this dude I worked with named Jorge. He was tall, very attractive, and a professional model. I was instantly drawn to his sense of style and the way he carried himself; that boy had swag. He was from the hood and lived in the Bronx. I wasn't comfortable giving him my virginity, so we pretty much did everything except for penetration. To me, his body was perfect, and our chemistry was always on point. He was effervescent and had a great sense of humor. Our sexual encounters always ended with us sharing anecdotes and life stories.

My preference has been to have sexual relationships with men I know and trust. A lot of that has to do with growing up being taught that all men ever want is sex. I liked to think that I had more to offer. So I made sure I provided more. Jorge was really into porn, particularly a genre that is problematically titled "chicks with dicks." The only time I've ever watched this type of pornography was with him. He was open about it. I appreciated that. He had desires that were largely rejected and judged by the community we are a part of. I later came to accept that I had a couple of my own.

The real issue I had with Jorge was that he was married with a family. The man had one son and his wife was pregnant again! He assured me he'd developed deep feelings for me and went out of his way to see me. But clearly it was a messy situation. I didn't really understand it; he didn't seem unhappy or even remotely interested in leaving his home. He was a man that wanted to escape his life temporarily through me. But this wasn't something I was willing to take or capable of taking on as a young woman exiting her teens, with very little experience with men and dating. So Jorge and I didn't last. Towards the end, after we had been involved for a few months, I remember him warning me about the dangers of rushing into marriage—something that definitely stuck with me.

I lost my virginity in my next significant relationship with a man named Olamide. I remember the first time I actually had sex: It was a stormy Saturday afternoon in Harlem. I was drunk off of Colt 45 and there was a Robin Thicke album playing in the background. It was actually sort of perfect. We had been dating for a couple of months. He was so handsome that it was sometimes hard for me to believe he was flesh and blood. He had decided to leave a very successful career in fashion and throw himself completely into his art. Olamide had travelled the world, been on billboards, and established himself. He was African but grew up in America, like me. What attracted me to him most was that he was an artist. He painted, wrote poems, and performed spoken word. Unfortunately, the passion he demonstrated in his art didn't translate into the bedroom. The sex was kind of stale and his stamina wasn't great. As a matter of fact, I imagined that's what sex might be like with an old man. I found those things disappointing, but I had feelings for him, so I powered through the deprivation and accepted the measly sexual scraps that came my way.

When it came to sex, he was very traditional. Our sex felt standard and routine. The one thing that I appreciated about sex with him most was that he always used a condom. It didn't matter how hot and heavy it got or how familiar we were with each other, or that I had only ever had sex with him. If there wasn't a condom, we weren't having sex. He once got an ex pregnant and the trauma of the abortion ordeal seemed to affect him greatly. Looking back, I'm grateful, because the importance of wearing a condom stayed with me.

He started getting shady when the career in art he'd dreamed of was not becoming a reality. Things weren't great, but I figured it was just the way things go. A relationship has ups and downs. But nope, he was stepping out on me. He met an older woman who offered to take care of him. So he moved in with her and ended it with me. He dropped me like nothing! I resented him for a while, but I eventually got over it. I remember him as having a good heart and I'm glad he was the first person I had sex with. We have a great laugh about the past whenever we run into each other now. The vibes are always right, and now I think of him like a big brother.

Until my early twenties, I was somewhat sexually conservative. My friends often complained that I was "uptight." I had several close platonic male friends, and I seemed to naturally relate to men. Most of the guys I dated I met through friends or at work. I went out a lot with my friends to clubs and parties, but at the end of the night, I wasn't leaving to have sex with guys. I had one or two one-night stands out of curiosity, but I wasn't a fan. The idea of being touched by someone who didn't give a damn about me, who might be only trying to use me for the night, repulsed me. I needed a connection, even if it was a small one, before I felt comfortable being sexual. I preferred that my sexual partners have a simpatico and respectful energy, and I set very clear standards with guys that I was going to see. If he didn't show me respect, he didn't get sex, period.

As I got older, I started to learn a little more and my rose-colored glasses were finally yanked off. I began to realize I live in a world where many guys make a sport out of girls. My next sexual experience was with another African guy named Jean. He didn't have standout looks like the previous guys I'd dated, but his life was a lot more stable and his manner was very unassuming. Jean was finishing his masters at an Ivy League university and seemed to come from a family with money. He drove a luxury vehicle, lived alone, and never seemed to worry about much. He looked and seemed like a "good boy," but he wasn't. Looking back, he seemed sneaky and he was a little corny. The first time we hung out, I wasn't all that interested. He asked me to be his girlfriend and I rejected him, but we continued to see each other.

Jean had a scheme. He kept a condom underneath his pillow at all times. And always had a big bottle of Grey Goose that he would mix with ginger ale into a potent cocktail for me when I would come over. I started to feel more comfortable around him and viewed him as unthreatening. I became more open to him and more attracted, so we started having sex. The odd thing about him was that he wasn't particularly good at sex, but the sex was good. His penis curved a little to the right, so maybe it was all mechanics. I had the best birthday sex of my life with him. He knew how to cooperate and that made all the difference.

I remember floating home after that. Maybe it was the stellar sex, but I became infatuated with him, even though this was a guy that I initially rejected. Before long, it seemed that he, on the other hand, had moved on. I began sending him long intense text messages and showing up at his apartment making scenes. I found out from a friend that he was chasing a mutual friend of ours and taking her out to expensive dinners. He was a player! He later told me that he would refill the Grey Goose bottle with Devil Springs—a very high-proof vodka—to get girls drunk faster, and that it was something that he had been doing for years! Looking back now, I recognize this as predatory behavior. That was my first official lesson in how that kind of dude operates.

In retrospect, too, I realized that his pulling away from me made me more attracted to him. His unavailability helped me avoid fears I had about getting close to someone, but I still got the perks of being in a love story through all the drama, chaos, and fighting.

Tyler was the first white guy I had a sexual relationship with. Dude was athletic and hot, the type of hot that women of all races, types, and backgrounds were attracted to. He defied not being anyone's "type" because all types seemed to want him. And he knew the effect he had on people. Yet he didn't come across as arrogant or manipulative. He was just cool. He was also very well endowed! He changed my initial perception of white guys. I believed a lot of the stereotypes about white guys and was a little afraid of what I heard. But he eradicated them. Until Tyler, I had completely avoided getting serious with white guys. It was just unfamiliar territory for me. I had hung out with some pretty exceptional ones too, guys who seemed to have the world at their feet, who were attracted to me, and who went out of their way for me. But it never mattered because I wouldn't let it get past a certain level. Looking back, I would regret not taking any of them seriously and be astounded at how closed-minded I was. Tyler and I were so compatible, I sometimes forgot he was white. It might have been the familiarity that made some obvious differences and preferences I had just disappear.

The first time Tyler and I spent the night together, we didn't have sex, and I liked the fact that he was cool with that. Our relationship was dynamic because fifty percent of it seemed very primal, and the other fifty percent was friendship. The primal part was intense; we were constantly touching or in physical contact. We often stopped to make out in public and we sometimes had sexual encounters in the street. We were in a zone, a very exhilarating one. In many ways, the relationship tested my limits. Half the time we just kicked back and laughed a lot! And let me tell you, the sex was off the chain. He was kinky and open-minded . . . *very* open-minded. He turned me on to things I had never tried or imagined. He freed me in a sense, and I learned that sex didn't really need to have any rules. I was down to try whatever and so was he, as long as we were both satisfied. Things with Tyler were very different from my first. We had a great run, but eventually we drifted apart. Our fantasy bubble burst, but our sexual escapades taught me to see and understand myself differently as a woman.

All of my sexual partners and experiences, good and bad, have taught me more about myself and my needs. But while discovering a deeper sense of who I was, I became more and more disillusioned with men. I was encountering and dealing with a lot of immature men, and maybe I wasn't making the best choices. Relationships seemed to make no sense and I was often let down, sometimes even heartbroken. This sent me into a downward spiral. My sense of self-worth declined, and this affected my sexual behavior. Until Tyler, I had been with only three or four guys. Maybe I even took pride in that, but it seems that the unsteadiness of my dating life and the men who used me took its toll.

I threw my moral compass into the ocean and turned my back on everything that I had been taught to believe was right. Sex was less about exploration and more about escape. This was interesting for me. Because at the time I wasn't seeing things for what they were. I was going through a very obvious phase while at the same time fighting to break free from all the restrictions that were imposed upon me. It was conflicting, because I was searching to understand myself, my boundaries, and my worth.

This period was tough, but it gave rise to the self-assured woman I was becoming. This journey was crucial to me not only understanding but grasping my worth, holding on to it with my bare hands and keeping it safe. A worth that was totally defined by me and nobody else.

Backed Up Fast Forward

Fortunate, indeed, is the person who has discovered how to give sex emotion an outlet through some form of creative effort, for he has, by that discovery, lifted himself to the status of a genius.
—Napoleon Hill

"Who you fucking?" is a common conversation opener among my friends and acquaintances. My usual response is "nobody," and I am very okay with that. This is where I find my own liberation. We are a paradoxical society that is simultaneously very sex obsessed and sex repressed, yet it seems to me that sex itself isn't particularly well understood. I feel that I understand myself, but navigating my identities in relation to the outside world is something else entirely.

I often find myself being judged and reprimanded by people who I feel lack basic conceptions of respect for themselves and others. People who don't seem healthy to me, who try to convince me that sex is always healthy while making erroneous assumptions that my lack of frequent sexual activity represents a fear of sexuality. I laugh . . . if they only knew. What if my vagina is just a lot more arrogant than I am? What if her standards are just a tad bit higher?

Sex is something that I've always viewed as a release and a facet of self-expression and exploration. Something that should be uninhibited, pressure-free, and pleasurable. If I don't feel comfortable and trusting of the outcome, I'll simply pass. Is it my willingness to pass on it so easily that is troubling to people? Is that my defect? Sex is omnipotent. Its energy and effects start before and after the actual sex act. I'm not sure if there's any doctrine out there that explains the power of sexual energy. But to me, the true capacity of sexual energy is a whole universe, one that exists outside the realms of physical pleasure or carnalities and procreation.

I have had to reconcile my sexual patterns and identity with my place in the world in order to make sense of things. It isn't repressed sexuality blocking me and, although I'm naturally reticent overall, I'm not a prude or afraid of what I want. It seems to boil down very selfishly to evaluating the worthiness of my potential mate. Who is this person and what exactly am I giving over to them? Is it just my body? What are they giving to me? Lady Gaga once declared, "I have this weird thing that if I sleep with someone, they're going to take my creativity from me through my vagina." She was mostly ridiculed for this statement, but I thought it made sense. If babies can come out of vaginas, then why can't creativity?

Last summer, I did one of my spiritual fasts. I did this one for a couple of weeks. It's the traditional form of fasting that I was taught, growing up in an Islamic home. No food from sun-rise to sunset. Fasting is my go-to method of spring cleaning for my soul. The fast went well. A couple days after, I had sex with this guy and although it was bomb, I remember worrying if all the hard work I put in had just been stroked up out of my yoni and redistributed to this nigga. Damn . . . I ain't like him that much!

It may seem neurotic, but I think there are several layers to sex that aren't generally explored. Here in the U.S., we are usually taught about conception, prevention, and contraception in our adolescence. Some of us are taught how to deliver en-joyable sex on a performative level, but what about on a pan-oramic level? Or even a paranormal level? Very rarely are we taught about how this energy drives us, and what it means in relation to our identity. What about the power sex can hold? Or the different ways in which it manifests or the sexual magne-tism that some wear naturally? Its universe is as unlimited as our own.

Transmutation is defined as the action of changing or the state of being changed into another form. Napoleon Hill, writer of the best-selling self-help book *Think and Grow Rich*, writes about sex transmutation as a means of acquiring wealth and success. The key, according to Hill, is harnessing sexual energy into a drive that is focused on a goal. Hill stresses that there is no energy stronger than sexual desire. Sexual energy is bound-less and can be created infinitely. Through the quest for sex-ual gratification, people become extremely ambitious and can reach great creative heights. That is the potential power of sex. It's a summoning force.

Sexual energy is a power that lies dormant in many and can be extremely useful when focused in the right direction. What if this code, once cracked, could unlock one of the great-est secrets of the universe? I think the first step would be to understand one's own sexual energy first by gauging how your mind, body, and even spirit are affected when you don't seek to gratify it.

A prime example of sex transmutation is when athletes are advised to hold off on having sex before matches or games in order to have greater mojo during game time. That mojo can be channeled in many different outlets, goals, and endeavors. I picture the regular execution of this to be nothing short of mind-blowing. The creative field is a prime practice for it because you are required to be emotive and to dig deep.

One of my friends told me that the reason why he thought I was so expressive and insightful was due to my lack of regular sex —a sort of backed-up brilliance. This is something that I have also wondered about because of the singular focus I have when it comes to writing. Maybe my subconscious makes the decision to hoard my sexual energy and use it for something bigger and better. After all, I have to ask myself, is there anything more climactic for me than finishing a piece of writing that I am proud of and sharing it with the world? I don't think there is. It is actually greater than climaxing because it yields a feeling of triumph. I've had satisfying, mind-blowing, amazing sex, but I have yet to experience triumphant sex. Maybe writing is my own personalized, weirdo version of sex? Through a specific outlet and sense of purpose? Maybe this exists for everyone in one form or another. How does it exist for you?

I continue to explore my understanding of this sexual universe. If the implementation of your natural sexual energy is boundless and powerful, what would happen if a source of this energy was targeted and stolen from you—specifically, a part of your body? I have grown up around women and young girls who were circumcised. Female genital mutilation is a harrowing archaic practice that continues in parts of Africa. The practice is based on the belief that when a girl's clitoris is removed, it extracts a part of her that is dirty and the source of her sexuality. I believe it's extremely dangerous, and it's largely viewed as inhumane. The girl could bleed to death, and I've heard of cases in which that occurs. The fact that there are societies willing to risk a child's life in order to prevent that child from growing into a fully sexually realized woman is incomprehensible and very telling.

Maybe they know that a woman's sexuality is a very potent and powerful thing. Maybe it is meant to be feared as a possible threat to the patriarchy. While I do not approve of this practice, I would describe the women I know who have experienced genital mutilation as strong and special. One of these strong, special women is someone I've known my whole life.

She is a mother and divorced. She told me once that she didn't crave or feel fulfillment from being a wife. She said that all that really matters to her is her family and the love, connection, and relationships she has with them. That has always been her main focus. Unfortunately, it seems to me that her family is mostly ungrateful, but she knows they need her. She is the oldest daughter and has been the primary breadwinner of her impoverished family in Africa. She came to the states, worked hard, and bought them a nice estate back home. She speaks to them every day on the phone and they depend on the money she sends. Without her, they would likely be living in the streets. Thinking about her experience has made me think about the possibility that the psyche might compensate for the loss of a vital part of one's being and body by developing another strength and another focus.

A couple years ago, I spent some time focusing on sex transmutation for spiritual and transformational purposes. I wanted to strengthen my aura and made a conscious decision to abstain from sex for several months. I've gone long periods of time without sex before, but I had never practiced purposeful abstinence. My goal was to build a strong aura since that is what I believe attracts positivity and great things. This is something that I discovered through fasting. Like clockwork, an obstacle appeared.

During this period, I was growing closer with a buddy of mine. It was a platonic friendship, but never in my life have I wanted anyone as much as I wanted this guy. He was so hot and oozed natural sensuality and magnetism. Damn! We were together all the time and I really enjoyed his company. In retrospect, his presence actually helped me with what I was trying to accomplish. Being around him produced a strong sexual energy within me. The repression of this desire and the growing tension produced the transmutation that had me walking around lit up and glowing. It was so obvious that people at that time made direct comments about my aura. I felt the radiance. This man was a never-ending source that I simply had to churn into what I needed. That was a major discovery for me.

There are whole ideologies and rituals based on cultivating male sexual energy. There are men who have sex and don't ejaculate or refrain from masturbation because they believe in the life force and sacred energy of sperm. There are people who believe in setting intentions and making visualizations with sexual partners before sex and climaxing with a common goal to be birthed like a baby. Sex magic. There are people who practice celibacy their whole lives as a sacrifice and expression of devotion to God. This practice is often associated with the Catholic faith and is becoming more and more controversial as time goes on. There are some people who capitalize off of their sexual energy and get paid for it. There are whole industries of mass consumerism that prioritize sex and the business of sex. From the realms of the spiritual to the mental to the physical and the capitalist, sex permeates them all. But as long as a woman has her own agency, sexual energy can serve as a beautiful force of natural alchemy. Don't let anyone tell you different.

Use what you got and then make some more.

Amina's Story

My teenage years were quite harrowing. Looking back, I realize I had a lot to overcome and never understood how to process my emotions. Sometimes I didn't even really understand the purpose of some feelings and why they mattered. I tucked them away years ago as a way of keeping myself safe from chaos and loss.

When I was in high school, our apartment building in Harlem burned down, and my mom and I lived in a shelter for about a year. To be fair, the shelter wasn't all that bad. It wasn't a big room with a bunch of bunk beds, as you might imagine. We had a small two-bedroom unit and we were really cool with the security guard. I was fine . . . at least, I felt fine. At that point, I had grown accustomed to my night terrors and I would relax by taking long walks down Lenox Avenue. That was my escape. I think my mom had a harder time. She seemed to be in constant emotional pain. She was stressed out to say the least, and things never seemed to get easier for her. She would often cry out, "When is my life going to change?" It broke my heart.

During this time, my aunt Amina returned to the city after marrying and moving to Maryland. She had gotten sick and came back to New York to be closer to us during this uncertain time. She was hospitalized at Harlem Hospital, a few blocks from where we lived. Amina was very special to me. She was about ten years older than me, so she was more like a big sister, and my mom raised her like a daughter. The two of them were the only family they had here when they left Africa. Amina took care of me most of my life until she got married. When I was around fifteen, my mother found Lambert, a very tall, handsome, West African man who wanted to marry Amina. He seemed like the perfect guy for her.

Amina was what you might call a "good girl." She didn't seem to have much real-life experience. At that point, she was in her mid-twenties, and her life revolved around us and the family friends she had grown up with. It was almost like she had been kept in a safe. A few years earlier, she had been seeing an African American guy, and they had even gotten engaged, but our family called off the wedding when he wanted to have sex with Amina before marriage. Amina seemed indifferent about it. This is how traditional my family was. Amina was the baby of the family and considered the angel, in an almost literal sense. She radiated goodness. So naturally, we were all very relieved when this second man came into our lives ready to marry Amina, and ready to wait to have sex until they were married. I'm not sure how Amina actually felt about all of this. I don't think she was ever really given a chance to explore her own identity or her own desires within all of the restriction. This was just how things were set up and how I knew them to be set up.

Personally, I thought the virginity thing was absurd. I always sort of had my own scenario in mind for myself regarding marriage and virginity. I definitely didn't plan on saving myself and I would let my fiancé in on it. When the time came, he would just have to lie to the family and bring them back a sheet stained with corn syrup.

For Amina, the wedding happened quickly. I remember her wedding day as an amazing and joyous experience for the family, especially for my mom. But it wasn't a good day for me; for some reason, I felt very sick. I almost passed out at the reception. I remember feeling drained and having to muster so much energy to pull myself together. Looking back, maybe it was my sadness and the realization that Amina wouldn't be with us anymore that had created a panic within me. The night after she settled into her married life, a huge honor was bestowed on the family: her husband confirmed that she was a virgin. In West African Islamic culture, it is a huge deal when the husband announces that his new bride was a virgin. My mother was honored because she was the one that raised Amina. And it was a great celebration for the family!

Amina moved in with her husband in Maryland, but she spoke to my mother every day. We were all very excited for Amina's new life and for the babies she would soon have. I went to visit her during my school breaks to catch up. She always sent me back home with a couple hundred dollars. I greatly appreciated the money at the time, because I was starting everything from scratch in that shelter. But as time passed, it seemed like Amina's life with her husband was very quiet, almost too quiet. Her husband would disappear at night sometimes, and I thought it was odd. I know Amina didn't like it, but she kept it to herself because she wasn't the confrontational type.

About a year and a half into their marriage, Amina's husband called to tell us that Amina was sick. I had a dream about her during that period. In my dream, she wasn't able to walk, and I was carrying her. It frightened me and seemed like an omen of what was to come. Amina came back to Harlem Hospital to be taken care of, and this was close to the shelter where my mom and I were staying. My mom would go there every day. I brought Amina Celine Dion CDs because they were her favorite.

Amina had beautiful hair that she took a lot of pride in. She had it treated and took supplements for it, but it was shaved off by the doctors. It was shocking and made me very sad.

One day when I went see Amina, I discovered that she had completely stopped speaking and interacting with people. A couple days later, I heard my mom on the phone hysterically screaming and crying and repeating "Amina's gonna die." The doctors told her that Amina had AIDS. I didn't understand this at the time, and it took me years to process. My mother never told anyone that Amina had AIDS. Pneumonia is what I was told initially, and that made even less sense to me. Later, I discovered that Amina contracted pneumonia because her immune system had weakened. She stopped speaking when she found out that she had AIDS. She knew death was looming and she just shut down. Everything she must have heard and known of AIDS was tragic, and she must've felt doomed. Amina was twenty-seven years old and had never had a sexual experience with anyone besides her husband, and here she was dying of AIDS. At this time, my mother and I were also dealing with being homeless and trying to rebuild our lives. Nothing felt real. Our life had imploded.

My mother never talked about the diagnosis and didn't tell anyone what killed Amina. Everyone thought she died from cancer. A part of me even believes that my mother convinced herself of that same lie. I chose to believe it myself for many years because the truth was just too painful, too real, too tragic. No one deserves to die like this; Amina didn't deserve this. After the funeral, the only time my mom mentioned Amina's husband was months later when she told me that he had been hospitalized. I didn't ask for any further details. I knew what it meant. The night after we had gotten the news of Amina's death, I had another dream about Amina. I was in a bus and she appeared and sat next to me. I looked at her and started crying hysterically and then she disappeared. In this dream, I didn't have to carry her.

After Amina's death, I was wracked with guilt. It didn't seem fair to me that she was dead, and I was still here. I spent several years running away from the pain of losing Amina. I held myself back and I struggled a lot. There was also a powerful feeling of shame that surrounded the circumstances of Amina's death. She died of a very real epidemic that we would never have imagined her facing in a million years. She was a "good girl" who never had casual sex or engaged in intravenous drug use. She watched funny movies with me, listened to her Whitney Houston CDs, and looked out for her family. Yet AIDS did not discriminate. Years later, and because of Amina's death, I really began to process the magnitude of this epidemic. The sad truth is that HIV and AIDS has hit Black women hard! I have read that, according to the Henry J. Kaiser Family Foundation, among all women, Black women account for the largest share of new HIV diagnoses (4,114, or 58% in 2018), and the rate of new diagnoses among Black women (23.1 per year) is 14 times the rate among white women.

Subconsciously, I think this tragedy made me very careful in matters involving sex. I don't have unprotected sex ever. In fact, it's something that is utterly terrifying to me. I miss Amina, and I am finally working on facing her death on a deep level. My heart is forever broken because of her loss. It often scares me to think that this will be a void within that I will always struggle to heal. But the best thing I learned from this was to allow myself to feel the pain and to process the experience in real time. I now realize that we didn't do Amina any favors by keeping her in a box and sheltered in white light. We don't do any girls any favors by doing that. What were we keeping Amina safe from? We threw her to the wolves.

I believe her death was God's will and should be accepted

as such, but I feel that her tragic death also highlights a very dangerous myth. This illusion of the chaste woman is a result of a society that purifies women into ignorance. As protective and cautious as I am with myself, I abhor the notion of being anybody's "good girl." I hate the term and everything it represents. The world doesn't need any more good girls.

MY BLACK EXPERIENCE

LightWORKER

*Everybody wants to be a nigga
but nobody wants to be a nigga.*
—Paul Mooney

In describing the arduous struggle of women to attain equality, legendary entertainer Bette Midler posted a shockingly insensitive tweet that read, "Women, are the n-word of the world." [sic] Naturally, this disturbed a lot of folks and caused a huge amount of backlash on both Twitter and in the mainstream media. What baffled me most was Midler's brazen sense of entitlement. It legitimately blew my mind that she had absolutely no regard for the countless horrific historical accounts associated with the word, and seemed completely oblivious to the weight and emotional impact of its use. Midler tried to justify her tweet by saying that it was a song by John Lennon and Yoko Ono from almost forty years ago. But it was a problematic declaration then, and most certainly still is today. Even in the context of provocation—of which I am a proponent through my platform—this still wasn't okay. It fell in line with all the fuckery and themes of white-womaning that have become more prevalent in this Trump era. In all its "social thriller" realness, like something straight out of a Jordan Peele movie, first they call the cops on us and then in an epic twist, when it serves their interests to be seen as oppressed, they *become* us. They seem to be displaying an obsession with and implicit sense of urgency regarding all things Black. Sound the alarm! Apparently, we all need to wake up and realize that women are being niggerized!

This comparison occurred again, and this time it came from a controversial, yet lesser known, white male comic named Josh Denny. Denny felt marginalized by society and used the same approach of drastically offensive fuckery. Journalists were constantly highlighting white men every time they committed acts of terror and Josh was tired of it! He expressed his frustrations into the Twitterverse and posted this doozy: " 'The straight white male' has become this century's N-Word."

Mic drop!

Just like that, the most historically problematic and privileged group of people on the face of the earth began forming an oppression narrative. Straight white male niggers. In all its glorious irony, they were trying to take back the N-word and own it. Entitled white comics co-opting the N-word. This was all some next-level shit and I couldn't process it. I would have to leap out of my own Blackness, skirt past my evolving consciousness, and work my way down a rabbit hole, only to arrive at a white-washed wonderland where I'd still be lost as fuck! But what it did do was open my eyes. It made me realize just how easily people were willing to make analogies that highlight the pain of the Black experience but never the glory, sacrifice, and strength of Black people. Ain't that some shit? I feel the need to counter that! If you wanna know what a nigger is to the world,

I'll let you know in my own tweetable way right here: Niggers are the lightworkers of the world! That's the type of provocative analogy that I want to promote. This is my absolute nigger truth. If you're gonna use the N-word, use it right.

I was first introduced to the term "lightworker" about a decade ago through one of my wellness-fanatic friends. I was fascinated by the term and through research, speaking with others, and gathering insight over the years, I began to uncover the meaning of *lightworker* on my own. In short, a lightworker is a torch carrier. Lightworkers represent a portion of the population that are born with a special mission to guide others into a better world. Eventually I learned that there is a very real distinction between bearing a light and being an active lightworker. The difference entails doing something with what you've got.

As rewarding and beautiful as this may all seem, the path of the lightworker is usually an alienating and difficult one. It is an existence that requires a lot of reconciling with the fact that one may never need or want what the world is telling you to want or need. On a grounded level, I would simply interpret lightworkers as people who are focused on the greater good. They are seeking to serve a purpose that's advantageous to the entire world as well as those around them.

As lightworkers became a trendy new-age topic, shallow-minded individuals with a self-serving agenda began pushing the notion that they were now glowing with chosen light. To my mind this seemed tantamount to piracy—spiritual piracy. Like they were offering a bootleg, street-corner, commodified version of spirituality. But my cynicism was countered as I met people who actually embodied all the ideals of lightworking, inspired and evolved souls. It wasn't about how they appeared to others or mass success. It was about the effect of individual impact on people's lives and forming community. Using your

God-given light to lead others along. Not a consumer-ready fix and product. People from all backgrounds navigating their way through life but with wider consciousness, understanding, and spirit-based insight than most. These are the kind of people we need more of.

Why are Black people lightworkers of the world? Because it's the absolute nigger truth. America was built through four hundred years of free labor and two hundred pounds of cotton picked daily in the blazing sun. Hands, muscles, bodies, and movement. Nigger light, nigger labor.

Yes, there is a resounding spiritual component to black survival in America and in the entire world. A component that's seldom examined and needs to be discussed more in mainstream conversation. Perhaps what would help propel this understanding is a vested interest in ancient belief systems. The light source. The light carried through generations and activated through the work of brave and brilliant Black people. How did Harriet Tubman read the stars without any formal education or astronomy background? The work of this woman is more profound than just a figure in Black history. She looked to save people while having a source of extraordinary enlightenment. As far as I'm concerned, her face shouldn't just be on a twenty-dollar bill, it should be on religious candles as well.

The lightworkers now are people empowering the world significantly through causes and active solutions, people on the front lines of justice crusades. People making innovative contributions of cultural significance. People who exemplify strength and possibility. All of these people carry a light that can activate into fire when necessary to destroy negative constructs and rebuild the new.

Les Cousins

Nobody wins when the family feuds
—Jay-Z, "Family Feud"

Les cousins translated from French into English means "the cousins." The dictionary defines *cousin* as one belonging to the same extended family. Any African will usually tell you that cousins are something we are accustomed to. Our families are often big. As an American African, however, I want to explain that this term goes beyond referring to family members. *Les cousins* is how Francophone Africans refer to African Americans in the U.S.

As a child, I didn't understand the connection between the literal meaning of the term and the projected identity of African Americans, but I always understood that the context was negative. It existed on a spectrum: from snarky description to sheer disappointment upon watching a young Black American man in a crime-related news story. It was most commonly used as a warning against going down the wrong path.

But despite the negativity, there was a clear understanding of a deep connection in there somewhere. After all, these were Black people like us. We saw them as a part of the same tree, just far off by the branches and much further away from their roots.

"*Les cousins* are always getting into trouble" was often stated, then followed by a disapproving headshake that stung of pity. The othering of African Americans by certain Africans is jarring to me. There exists a Yoruba word that they associate with African Americans, *akata*.

Akata means "wild cat." A cat without a home. A stray. This is a term that I find deeply

disturbing and foul. *Akata* may be a lot more extreme than "the cousins," but whether we are talking about a stray cat or an extended family member, the message is clear—we are not the same and do not share a home.

Historically, "brother" or "sister" has been considered a universal term of solidarity between Black folks. But when one group of Black people decides to cut the cord and refer to only a select few, a few like them, as their siblings, and to refer to the rest as just their cousins, it's a troubling thing.

When I was in ninth grade, one of my teachers was giving a lesson on

Africa and discussing the poverty rates. One of my classmates responded with, "Fuck Africa," and went on a rant about why Africans deserve everything they are experiencing now for selling their own to Europeans. He stated that Africa was experiencing karma. I was gobsmacked and hurt by this. I thought of the degree of poverty I have witnessed in Africa, refugees from Liberia who fled to neighboring countries because of atrocious war conditions. Girls my age who lived and worked as housemaids making the equivalent of forty bucks a month.

I thought of a little girl who had jumped on the side of our car to beg for money and the look of gratitude she gave me when I gave her my spare change. This was a level of genuine gratitude that I as a teenage girl was grossly unworthy of. I thought about my own cousin who had been raped during war in Liberia, had her chest burned and her brother murdered in front of her. I thought about a woman back home, in Guinea, who had brain cancer and still had to go to work every day. I thought about the misery and the realities of just how fucking hard life could be.

I asked my father about what my classmate said. My father was a very knowledgeable man. He had been a diplomat until he fell out with the government, and then later he became an antique art dealer. I always valued his insight. He explained to me that slavery was something that has always existed in Africa within tribal wars and battle, but what the white man had done with slavery was an abominable evil that wasn't anticipated. We didn't know what we were selling our people into and the horrors that awaited them.

This topic was something I've been confronted with several times in different forms. Usually it has been by African Americans telling me condescending things that they had heard about Africans. But it was never a conversation I was willing to have. I knew that most of these statements weren't meant to create any sort of dialogue to grow and learn from. And I didn't want to place myself in a position to confirm or deny them. What was I supposed to do? Act like a lot of other Africans and downplay this very obvious fact about African slavery? How was this any different from how white Americans handle discussions of race in America? Or would I just become defensive and fall back on the issues that Africans have with African Americans instead, issues that I didn't even feel entirely aligned with myself? As one Black person doing this to another Black person, wouldn't this somehow be worse? On one end of the spectrum, there were pompous and ignorant assessments of African Americans made by Africans. And on the other end, I had to deal with resentful or ignorant assessments of Africans from African Americans. If ever there was a thing as Black fragility, I'll tell you, these things certainly triggered it within me.

The fact was, I was a Black girl in America with African parents. I didn't know that much about the African American experience beyond this. All I really knew were my friends and the shit I learned in school, which was one-dimensional and borderline insulting. I needed to learn more, so I started reading more books on my own.

From Black supremacist theory to slave narratives to content on colorism and its history, I learned a lot and it opened my eyes. It dispelled my own ignorance, and forced me to call out the ignorance, unfairness, and division I saw in others. But I decided to fully reckon with this when I saw *Black Panther*. Ironically, as vital as *Black Panther* was in terms of Black representation in film, it didn't do much to properly address the strife and tension between us. Killmonger and T'Challa were in fact cousins: the African American and the African.

As I was watching, I saw the larger context of my own Black American experience and the collective anger that Killmonger represented. Why did these Africans have to win, and Killmonger have to lose? Why did "le cousin" have to be killed off? Wouldn't it have been a reaffirming message if they got through to Killmonger? To me, Killmonger was portrayed as an *akata*, the wild stray the Wakandans didn't want in their home. As much as I loved this movie promoting African pride and the enchanting greatness of Africana, having an African American villain and a noble African savior didn't strike me as progressive. But this was a comic-book movie, so it really didn't have to be.

As Africans in America are trying to carve their paths as model minorities, they seem to revel in the distinction that they are not the same as their African American counterparts. They often seem proud to be seen as Black people who are "different." Accepting that societal pat on the head can seem to open doors and put them above the fray in their eyes. But does it really? I don't think it's putting anyone above the fray so much as it is showing indifference and apathy towards the advancements of others. A small number of Africans who come to America to hone themselves and generate wealth and opportunity will eventually go back to their home, their land, and their people. And for the most part, I don't think they are seen as a real threat to any preservationist white American agenda. Very rarely do you find these recent African immigrants fighting to tear down any monuments and shake up the system. Their history is different with this country. They weren't brought here in chains. And now they are gaining what they came for in America. Frankly, they are too caught up in hustling for their families in Africa to really focus on the issues here.

In my experience, African millennials who arrive in this country have a superiority complex that I do not see with American Africans, those born and raised in America to African parents. Those of us who were born in the United States and grew up here seldom see ourselves as being much different from any other Black person here. We are often struggling to express our own unique identities to our families and to African society. I don't really relate to African millennials that arrive in America, and I believe one of the main reasons is that I am far less traditional and a lot more open-minded than they are.

At the end of the day, you have millions of people from countless nations all over the world represented here in America, many of whom have their own derogatory terms for African Americans and consider them inferior. Many are shamefully ignorant of the fact that it is the suffering and struggle of African Americans that made America what it is and allows them to be here today. The trauma, the tragedy, and the scars that are held by the descendants of the people that actually built America are forever present and don't just disappear. It blows my mind to see the truth of these struggles erased in anyone's eyes.

A real dialogue is necessary so that the entire diaspora can understand the pain of the others. As powerful, majestic and great as Africa is, it is largely ravaged by poverty, disease, and a history of unrelenting corrupt officials and dictators. The land was imperialized, raped, and left for dead by European conquests and transgressions. The disconnect lies in the veil that has been created between the African American experience, the African experience, and the world.

The African immigrant experience in America is characterized by a sense of urgency and drive. The drive comes not just from our African roots giving us some sort of advantage, but from the support of a family structure which hasn't been torn apart by centuries of rampant white hostility separating families and preventing what is necessary for true self-expression.

For some Africans, the stability of an educated nuclear family paves the way for a new generation that is educated and stable. All the Africans I know in the U.S. fit somewhere in that paradigm, a paradigm that promises a greater chance of success. For me, however, it's different. I never had an extreme drive to succeed unless it truly meant something to me. That's something I had to search for on my own, free of obligation. But I can't deny that there is an effect in knowing and witnessing how people live in the U.S. versus Africa. I see this as my American privilege, as well as my odd internal African privilege.

Whether you are an American African who considers the U.S. your home, or you are an African immigrant who is benefiting from the struggle of the slaves who built this country, the right thing to do is to put in the work to build up the community and the society both back in Africa and in the U.S. The basis of the most culturally relevant movements, trends, and institutions in this country rests on the backs of Black Americans. Period. The world often overlooks what is being birthed by Blacks here. It is their strength, soul, and resilience that cultivated all of this. And it is the same strength, soul, and resilience that can be found in all melanated peoples throughout the entire diaspora. Same sap, same tree. We can't be afraid of uncomfortable dialogue, and we can't allow the system that separated the family to keep the family apart.

All This Talking Shit

Don't waste your time with explanations: people only hear what they want to hear.
—Paulo Coelho

Debates are an exciting and necessary source of stimulation for me. Arguing, hurling insults, and getting offended, however, are not. It is vital to distinguish whether you are growing in consciousness as a result of intellectual verbal sparring or just getting gathered and having your energy drained. The bottom line is: Is this a debate or an argument? I don't like arguments, so I don't do them. If there isn't some sort of mutual goal of reaching a solution or at least finding common ground—just miss me with all this talking shit. If you wanna vent get a diary, because I learned from experience never to engage in open-hearted conversation with close-minded people.

Racial debates in this country add some extra heat to my

already boiling pot. Debates, arguments, and heated discussions are a constant occurrence in this era. We are told that things are coming to a head and that the truth is being exposed now.

Politics makes strange bedfellows indeed. Either we are joined together and forced to awaken to the deep-seated racist realities of America, or joined together to gag and swallow on the thriving and progressive multidimensional face of the new America. Because the pillow talk is real out here!

But what happens after one of these debates or arguments end? Are you swayed by anyone? Is your mind opened? Have you, a leftist liberal, gotten a Trump supporter to see the light, put their MAGA hat down, and join hands with all of us at the foot of the rainbow? Has that raging conservative managed to convince you that Black Lives Matter is a terrorist organization and the country needs to keep Mexicans and "illegal" immigrants out by any means necessary?

Has all of this talking shit gotten us anywhere? I'm asking, seriously.

Because if you're anything like me, chances are that one of these incidents left your blood pressure skyrocketing as you walked away truly disappointed in society. We live in a time when dialogue is necessary—for planning, for expressing our pain, and for supporting one another. But is all dialogue healthy? It's a fallacy that we must talk and come to terms with the opposition.

Should I subject myself to this? Politicians are getting paid to take on oppressive forces and negotiate with them. Well-informed pundits are being hired to present two well-informed sides. I, however, am not! All this back and forth feels futile and costs me energy that I am, frankly, no longer willing to give.

The Obama-era racial debates often consisted of lip service from a lot of white liberals—a group of people who strike me as being pretty out of touch. Some of the most heated debates I have had about race were with these lip-service liberals. To me, this sort of white liberal often seems well insulated in a bubble of "Kumbaya." But perhaps they are actually the dirty underbelly of humanity. They talk the Kumbaya bullshit but can't engage in a meaningful conversation about racial issues because they don't have much to say. In short, these white liberals don't want to deal with it, so they don't.

I have vivid recollections of people who have never been Black a day in their lives telling me how America responds to and treats Black people. I remember one guy in particular (a proud Democrat and two-term Obama voter, by the way) saying to my face that I was making up and exaggerating the state of racism in America when I told him about "Shopping While Black." This was something he had never heard of.

I explained to him that Black people get profiled and followed around in stores regularly. I was explaining this because I was trying to get him to understand the emotional and mental effects this has on us. Shopping while Black can cause anxiety when you realize that you are being watched closely and constantly while just casually browsing. Some people avoid certain stores because of this, or will only set foot in them when they're sure they're going to buy something. This man proceeded to whitesplain to me that all of this was ridiculous. That should have been my cue to stop wasting my time and my words, but I didn't because I was insulted. How could you tell someone that what they have experienced is bullshit?

The conversation got heated and ended with him telling me that I am what's wrong with America. "It's people like you," is how he started that sentence. He whitesplained some more that it wasn't racism that was the issue, but instead it was people like me who harp on it and make mountains out of molehills. *This* was his interpretation of what I shared. By informing him of my experiences, making him conscious of "Shopping While

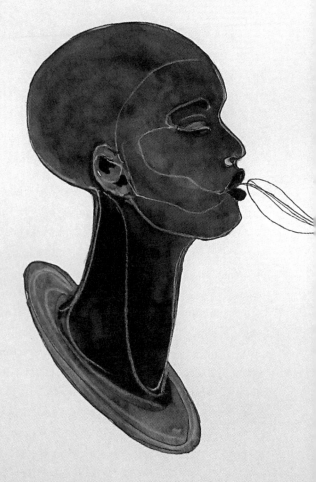

Black," and defending my point of view, I, a Black woman, became the problem with America.

This man seemed unable to hear the truth because it triggered feelings and realities that he wasn't prepared to face.
Things that he thought a Black president would easily soothe
away. I guess he wasn't ready for this shit. If he couldn't handle
this, imagine how he would handle being followed around a
store as a Black man or being "randomly" stopped by the cops to
be frisked and demeaned (which is something that every Black
man I know in NYC has experienced).

One thing is, during this post Obama era, I seldom encoun-

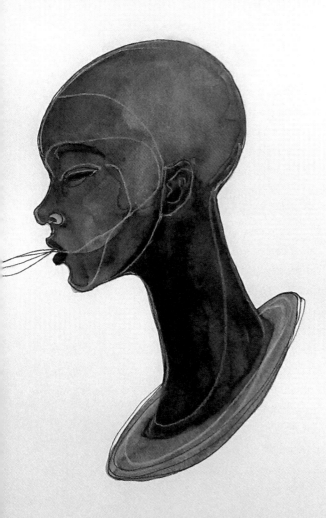

ter any vocal ultra-conservative Republicans. This might have to do with the fact that I live in a blue state and they kept that shit on the down low. The few Republicans that I met would just immediately dismiss me by saying, "You don't understand politics." As if their understanding of "politics" was more valid than my lived experience. I know fuckshit when I see it, and politics in general is agenda-based fuckshit. These dismissals by both Republicans and Democrats started to get to me. I wondered if I was, in fact, crazy. I kept being told by white men that I was "off" about racism. What I thought were simple observations about the state of race in America were always countered with some form of lashing out. I might not have been crazy, but I was definitely missing something, and that was that having an honest talk about race with a Black person was taboo for a lot of white people. Imagine that; a country with such an extreme racist history flowing through every artery of American life, and I was just supposed to shut up about it. This tone policing shows how easy it is to be suddenly turned into the attacker or angry Black bitch. Demand justice and be labeled as part of a hate group. So I had to suppress all my thoughts to coddle and accommodate a collective white fragility that was actually rooted in a pathological greed and desire for dominance.

Those lip-service liberals seem to have been somewhat silenced by the irrefutable. Trump was voted in, and it seemed that a sea of angry bros was emboldened and came out of hiding. Suddenly, these liberals became incensed with foul-truistic rage! They are having Rachel Maddow–style breakdowns while running around rabid with severed Trump heads and declaring, "This isn't the America I know."

Did you catch that? Susan's had an awakening! Gee, where the fuck you been, Susan? Oh yes, that's right! You were Kumbaya-ing at the foot of that rainbow with the rest of the deluded bunch. I'm glad you finally arrived! Better late than never. Now get a grip.

Now, in the Trump era, racial debates surround me with latent racists and their apologists. I am being hijacked and baited into arguments by people who are just looking for a Black person to whom they can express their issues with Black America. I feel cornered and used. The same people who claim that all white people aren't the same are the ones turning me into the Black American representative.

I was at a party once and this dude decided to bring up slavery. He goes, "Why are Black people still upset about slavery? It happened a long time ago." I took the bait. How is any

Black person expected to react to this without getting sucked in? It's an antagonistic trap! He was clearly looking for a fucking fight. He got one that day, too.

But again, it proved to be a waste of time for both of us. He took out his anger on me while denying his own racism. This argument escalated to him claiming that the cops were well within their rights to shoot unarmed Black men, because after all, we don't know the full story and Black people shoot each other too!

Once again, this heated conversation ended with him saying to me, "Its people like you," yada yada. A white man in America in denial of the country's atrocities was once again telling me that I was actually the problem. People like me who aren't over racism. But people like me are logical and can't be mansplained or whitesplained to. A thinking Black woman or a stupid Black girl can hold her own in discourse and challenge you. And you think I'm the problem?

One evening, I met up with my friend Blaine. I met him in the nightlife scene. Blaine is a very cool, popular Black dude in the city. I met up with him at a bar, and that night he was with one of his standard pretty blonde girls.

I had never met this girl before and right off the bat she was talkative and tipsy. I didn't feel comfortable with how assertive she was with me. I like meeting new people, but I don't like too much familiarity too fast. That's the energy this girl was giving me. In the middle of my first drink, she asked me to take her to the bathroom. I told her I was fine sitting where I was. She then implored drunkenly, "I'm just a poor little white girl, I can't do it myself." I was stunned.

Blaine's bartender friend looked at the both of us, and I had to make a decision how to handle this. Did this bitch think I was her mammy? I had never heard anyone come out of their face like that. That comment was simultaneously demeaning to her, and disrespectful and racially loaded towards me. I tried something different. I ignored it, even though I was being poked with a stick. Here I was just trying to meet up for fucking drinks with one of my boys, and this dumb bitch had already tried it like thirty minutes in.

The bartender lived in the neighborhood and invited us all to chill and smoke out at his place. I don't smoke weed, but I wanted to chill. Aside from that comment, I was having a cool summer night and wanted to be around people. On the cab ride over, Blaine and this girl were talking about a racist incident with the cops that had occurred the week before. The girl kept saying how shaken up she was by it, how unfortunate racism is, and how it hurt her to see her friend in that situation. This girl had already given me one red flag at the bar. This was another.

I had only known her for an hour or two, and race had been brought up directly twice. It was clear to me that race was an issue for her. I learned that she lived on the Upper East Side and had just left a physically abusive relationship with a very wealthy man, which seemed to have traumatized her. Apparently, she was desired by a lot of wealthy conservative men, and she had hung out several times with her ex at Trump's Florida resort, Mar-a-Lago. She was a hot blonde, a hot commodity out here. She attracted these men like honey, but that had ultimately come with a big price. She seemed to be in a fragile state that night.

The topic of race came up again after recounting the racist incident with Blaine, herself, and the cops. She seemed to feel the need to affirm to me that she wasn't racist. I was annoyed, so I took the bait. I reminded her what she had said in the bar earlier about being a "poor little white girl" who needed me to help her to the bathroom. I told her that everything about that remark was problematic and offensive. I tried to remain calm because I had been in situations like this before, when latent racists get called out on their shit. I knew that it was important to remain calm to get a good look at what was going on with their spirit when they were triggered and confronted. And lo and behold, it became clear, because she *lost her shit.* "Are you calling me a racist?!" she shouted. I calmly informed her that what she said was offensive and inappropriate. She got angry and started crying! We had a tense exchange during which she was flipping her shit and causing a scene. I tried to remain logical with her. She called me an asshole and asked me why I was calling her a racist. I told her that she was crying because I was a holding a mirror to her face and showing her the truth of the situation, and it was so ugly that it made her cry.

She might've been ignorant, but at the end of the day, her spirit knew the truth. I know that she knew. After I told her that, she got even more upset. And I got annoyed. This girl had insulted me in the bar and now was having a full meltdown because I was expressing to her that her behavior was not okay! She couldn't listen, learn, or grow. She had to victimize herself. But I also actually felt sorry for her. She had confided in me about her abusive relationship and seemed vulnerable. This situation was getting complicated. I decided to stop, because this girl wasn't going to get it anyway—at least not at this moment. The bartender whose apartment we were in was starting to get upset as well. He had been so hospitable, and I didn't want to disrespect his space.

Racism, and specifically this kind of casually racist behavior, is almost a disease to people like this girl. It felt like confronting an alcoholic about their alcoholism or staging an intervention. Shit can go left and folks don't want to face the truth about who they are because they aren't ready to change. I took a deep breath and accepted that. We continued with the evening. As I talked more with this girl, I found out that she was actually very spiritual. She had a lot of answers and even taught me some spiritual tools. I found it ironic, but apparently there was more to her. To be honest, this result would typically take too much for someone like me to get to.

But somehow, I ended up being divinely patient and compassionate that night. It would take too much effort as a human and as a Black woman for me to look past her behavior and her lashing out. I don't owe that to anyone. It's also a gamble. I'd have to live with myself and my conscience knowing that I didn't express myself and check her the way I should. What was she letting go of to meet me at this peaceful place? Nothing. We are always taught that we need to change the world through compassion when it is seldom ever extended towards us. Everybody ain't Karamo Brown! I'm not always readily equipped with the divine spirit I carried that night. But I learned something.

A year later, I found myself in a similar situation. I was hanging out at a house party, and I met this girl named Amy. She was a cool brunette from Kansas who liked horror movies like me. We hit it off and were having great conversation. Later, she got in a political argument with the friend who'd invited me. She revealed that she was a Trump supporter and expressed her thoughts on immigrants and Black Lives Matter. But this time I refused to take the bait. I stepped away from them and went into another area of the room where I watched from a distance. They were talking for a while, and I saw my otherwise chill friend become combative. I went back to support my friend but said nothing. Amy continued bashing Black Lives Matter. That was a trigger for me.

I didn't want to argue, so I tested my divine approach once more. I thought she may just be ignorant and uninformed. I tried to make her understand that Black people have an emotional response to oppressive systems and history because we've been hurt by them. We are angry and want change. I felt like I was explaining empathy to a five-year-old. She brushed my words off as whining and self-pity. To me, it seemed like she didn't want to hear what I had to say because it wasn't even her talking. She sounded almost like a robot; like she was repeating ideas she'd been fed and accepted without any thought. Amy got angry, but I had been through this before, so this time I didn't bother wasting any emotion. But I was shaken by the fact that a civilized, patient, and empathy-driven debate had not moved her in the least.

Later that night, the party was winding down and I was chatting with the host. We discovered that we had both lost our fathers, and it was comforting to hear his story. His father had died of cancer. Amy came over and joined our conversation and told us about her father, who died in a car accident when she was eighteen. The three of us got into a very emotional conversation. The host was telling us how he had reached a point of acceptance, and I shared a similar feeling. Amy didn't seem to have gotten to that point. She still seemed to be going through a very hard time and started crying over her father. He had been her best friend, and the wound of his loss was still very fresh for her. We offered her comfort and support. She was a girl dealing with the pain of losing her father, just like I had. But again, it took a lot for me to get to all this. I had to be patient and divine. I didn't owe her that. But I learned something.

I learned that what we are facing at the moment is often much more complicated than we realize. I learned that we are all humans, but that we are less likely to see that in each other with all that we are facing right now. I learned that I don't owe anyone that amount of patience and divine response, but that it is up to me to decide when to exercise it. And I still struggle with it sometimes. I learned that although all these race-related conversations, debates, and arguments may not change our opinions, there is a possibility of a future where we could at least see each other differently. We aren't there yet.

Ultimately, these encounters were one-sided. I don't suspect either of those girls gained anything that they will put to use, but I hope that on some level they understand there is no real truth behind what they say or think regarding race. But that doesn't matter. They are making a decision within themselves not to grow and to perpetuate racism. I, however, have a greater understanding of my spectrum of humanity. I want people to open their eyes, to grow, to think, and to accept one another. But they have to want it for themselves!

They have to be open to sacrificing all the power and the privilege that they have in order for the world to be better. That's the bottom line. All this talking shit does is demonstrate the ignorance with which they are willing to fight for their privilege and power—a blissful ignorance that has been passed down to them. That is the biggest problem here. Can that be lifted and unveiled through a single debate or argument? No, it can't.

So I'll save my breath.

Blood and Soil

"Blood and Soil! Blood and Soil! Blood and Soil!" Angry white nationalist protesters chanted these words as they marched through Charlottesville, Virginia. The Nazi battle cry used by thousands of white men whose ancestors stole Native American land, enslaved and worked Black bodies for centuries for the privilege, control, and power that they now hold. Privilege, control, and power that they feel is not enough and being stripped by those they have always oppressed—a chant to reclaim a land that their forefathers had already claimed.

I was told from a very young age that blood should never touch the ground. Blood touching the ground signifies finality. The end. Blood touches the ground in war and defeat. For that reason, whenever I bled, I made sure to get it covered or elevated right away, because I am not ready to commit myself to any final unspoken universal oaths. But perhaps America is. In fact, it seems pretty clear that America is. This country has reached a peak.

Ancient ancestral African spirituality isn't commonplace in the United States. It has been eroded considerably by Christianity and colonialism. But, in fact, it is still very much alive in the world. In parts of Africa, Latin America, Haiti, and the Caribbean islands, some form of this is the primary faith that is practiced. And it's fundamentally the basis of Voodoo and Santeria.

Within the Yoruba/Ifa tradition, animal sacrifices are made to the other realm regularly. An exchange, mainly for the blood, is considered the purest symbol of life energy. Blood must spill for it to be sealed. Blood and soil. But the ancient cultural beliefs of African traditional spirituality are largely considered primitive, inhumane, and evil, and are regarded as witchcraft by much of the western world.

The concept of the animal sacrifice is part of Islamic tradition as well. During Eid (Festival of the Sacrifice), an animal is sacrificed and divided into three parts. It is to honor Ibrahim and his obedience to God in willingly sacrificing his son. Even though the meat is being eaten, one could argue that a deeper understanding and value of the animal can be found through such rituals. Every ounce and dimension of the chicken is utilized—from taste to totem. So when I heard those angry white people chanting in a unified outcry, I decided to explore connections and to look into America's history of exchanging blood for power.

The United States and European nations have historically travelled all over the world, conquering people for the sake of sovereignty. In those cases, chicken lives weren't the ones being exchanged for power—human lives were. The genocide of the Native Americans was a direct exchange for power. The murder and genocide that are an integral part of American history can be seen as ritualized acts of human sacrifice. So-called patriotic Americans believe these acts were necessary sacrifices in order for a group of people to stay at the top. It strikes me that even blue-blooded Americans who come from old money have their own superstitions and secret societies, like the Skull & Bones society, with their own ritualistic practices and traditions.

A few years ago, I was reading a Twitter exchange between rapper/singer Azealia Banks and Sia, the Australian singer/songwriter. Azealia had mentioned something about her own spiritual practices based on African ancestral traditions and how she, herself, sacrifices chickens. In my experience, this type of ritual is traditionally conducted by mediums. I personally had never heard of anyone sacrificing an animal themselves. But it seems that Azealia was conducting these rituals, and she was sharing it with the world.

Sia was outraged by these rituals, and she lashed out at Azealia in defense of the chickens. To me, Sia's judgmental argument seemed to be coming from a place of ignorance. Sia, and many of the others calling these rituals barbaric, were the beneficiaries of privilege and power gained through actions similar and far more extreme. And here she was crying over chickens. It also seemed right on time to me, since I've seen so many white people cry over a dead animal before they shed a tear or voice outrage over a slain Black body. Where were Sia's tweets on that?

Anyway, if blood and soil must perpetually meet in order for those in power to maintain their power, then this is in fact some type of spiritual law. The unjust attacks and cops murdering Black folks need to continue in order for this system to be fed. The blood has to constantly be hitting the floor. Is this why they were chanting? Is this what they feel threatened is coming to an end? As people of color are speaking up even louder now against all of it, these white people aren't gaining power anymore. They are losing it.

Now they are marching without their hoods and seem emboldened to do so. What is more reminiscent of witchcraft and satanism than the Klan itself? They have their own uniform, grand wizards and burning crosses, ceremonies and lynched Black bodies on trees all in the name of ritualized order. They scream "WHITE POWER!" for crying out loud! This was one of the main constructs of America's spiritual design. This was a belief system that millions of people had been a part of, in one form or another. This is White Power ritualized.

How does the sacrifice of some goats or chickens compare to generations of that? If spilling blood creates power, how much power does all that blood even equate to? I'll tell you. Inconceivable amounts of it. So why are they marching and angry? Damn. Was all that blood spilled *still* not enough to keep us down? And have America's own chickens finally come home to roost?

I'd say so.

Brown

I am not tragically colored.
There is no great sorrow
dammed up in my soul,
nor lurking behind my eyes. . . . Even
in the helter-skelter skirmish that is
my life, I have seen that the world
is to the strong regardless of a little
pigmentation more or less.
No, I do not weep at the world—
I am too busy sharpening
my oyster knife.
—Zora Neale Hurston,
Dust Tracks on a Road

My father was an antique African art dealer and dealt the art he collected straight out of our apartment. The main themes in our home were art and world politics. When people came over to visit, one of the two were always discussed over my mother's glorious African dishes.

My father truly loved and profoundly respected the art and seemed to take a lot of pride in it. He would share in-depth analyses of his pieces: the history, tribal origins, and selling prices. When he wasn't running around to galleries in the city, he was sitting at home waiting on clients and working on displays for hours at a time. It wasn't an environment that consciously strived to foster Afro-positivity, it just was. This was a way of life.

We lived on the Upper West Side of Manhattan, where my father had settled in the seventies and stayed after working as a Guinean diplomat in Egypt and Yugoslavia. Our apartment building was across the street from Central Park, right by the Dakota, the infamous building where John Lennon had lived with Yoko Ono and where Lennon was assassinated. The air in my home seemed rich with artistic energy. A nostalgic reverence for those creative minds was deeply ingrained within me. The building was in a great location. It had a doorman, and the accessibility of his apartment and neighborhood was great for my father's clients. He had a variety of them, from other dealers to wealthy collectors who sought him out specifically for his pieces.

My father was a connoisseur with an amazing eye for beautiful things, and an aesthetic rooted in his love of Africa. He would rip out pictures in magazines of regal, elegant brown women and save them in manila envelopes or leave them around the house between art books and magazines. I vividly remember seeing Naomi Campbell's "Got Milk?" ad among his assortment of black images.

From an early age, I understood my father's deep appreciation of Black female beauty. He saw value in it, and so I believed there was value in me as well. These women were mostly brown like me. I didn't have to convince myself that Black was beautiful, and I didn't need to convince anyone around me of it either. It didn't feel like an act of resistance or a campaign to prove anything to anyone. To me, Africana was life, and was a rich culture that I felt privileged to be in the middle of. This world shaped and defined my unique New York City coming-of-age experience.

After my parents split, I moved uptown to Harlem with my mother. But during our years in Harlem, I went to a high school in downtown Manhattan. It was a great school. The population was predominantly Latinx and Black students, with some Asian and very few white students. Thankfully, in this context, the commonly held conception of Black female inferiority seldom reared its ugly head.

I was fourteen the first time I remember encountering a "less than" vibe. A group of us were talking about dating, and one girl asked one of the Asian boys what type of girls he was into. His response was, "Anything but Black." He said it casually, even though a few of us in the group were Black girls. His response was received with indifference, as if he had just proclaimed that the sky was blue. And I was shocked.

The next instance I remember was when some of the boys made an anonymous list of the top ten hottest girls in school. All of the girls on that list were Latina with one exception—a mixed-race girl. The girl they picked as number one had the lightest skin, green eyes, and dyed blonde hair. This didn't go over well with the Black girls in the school, but nobody knew whom to blame. I didn't think too much about it at the time, mostly because I wasn't much of a hot girl in high school, so I didn't expect to be on that list in the first place. I had pink box braids, acne, and I guess I was sort of weird. But one thing did give me pause. The girl that they picked to be number one never even interacted with any of the Black boys at school. This girl paid none of these boys any mind and only communicated in Spanish with her clique, yet they still gave her the top spot. She didn't seem to give a fuck about their list and never even spoke about it.

I asked one of the boys at school about this list. His name was Jerrod, and he was big, about six foot four, with dark skin. He looked older and more like a bouncer than a high school student. He said he knew who made the list, and that they had chosen that girl because she was the prettiest and her eyes were amazing and green.

As I thought about it, I realized that this girl's physical proximity to whiteness as a Latina had a lot to do with the perception of her beauty. I admit, I also thought she was pretty. But she didn't fuck with anyone outside of her group in school. And I think that's what rubbed me the wrong way. In my eyes, here was Jerrod, this big Black kid, out here vouching for a girl who to him was unreachable. Aside from our teachers, she was the whitest person at our school, and her attitude seemed to make that even clearer. So Jerrod's remarks sounded ridiculous to me.

I recall having a conversation with Jerrod's best friend in which he told me that I would look better if I permed my hair and stopped wearing box braids all the time. He pointed at another girl to give me an example. Her hair was relaxed and straight with no body or bounce. I was confused. What was it that these boys were trying to make me understand about myself?

The interesting thing about that high school list is that I keep seeing it in different forms in the media, and they are essentially the same as the one those boys made. I thought of that high school list recently when I saw *Maxim* magazine's "Hot 100," a curated list of one hundred women considered the most attractive of the year. This high school list reappears all over the media in countless lists that exclude Black women. You see it in fashion and beauty pageants, the pattern of women who get all the buzz, and even when looking at the wives and girlfriends of the hottest entertainers. Through this exclusion, it is insinuated that Black women don't count when it comes to mainstream desirability or beauty. According to these lists, there are women and then there are Black women.

Black women are considered subpar and have to be A-list in order to appear on those kinds of rankings mixed in with C-list white starlets. Obviously, it's not that beautiful Black women don't exist in the world now, or that they were absent from my high school either. That list was my first glimpse at the denigration of Black female beauty, yet I managed to remain protected in my well-insulated, familial bubble of loving Blackness a bit longer. It wasn't until I was about nineteen that I really started to grasp how society views Black women and where we fall in the hierarchy. The first time was when I was working at a retail store. One night, a couple of us were discussing hitchhikers while closing up. One of the managers adamantly stated that there was no way, under any circumstances, that he would pick up a hitchhiker. One of the girls retorted, "What if she was a pretty blonde?" I remember genuinely not understanding how her being blonde mattered. I asked my coworker and her response was simply, "You know, a pretty blonde," as if I didn't hear what she said. Our manager seemed to get it because he didn't offer any argument after that. Maybe it was because his wife was supposedly a white blonde woman herself. He never brought her around, but that's what I heard.

What makes this even more significant was that the girl who gave the example was Black, and so was the manager.

Why would this Black man let this blonde hitchhiker's social capital skew his principles, knowing how the system worked? Why continue to grant privilege to others that is not extended to us? I didn't understand how or why I was supposed to see more value in this hypothetical blonde than in my coworker or myself.

I remember another incident during my retail stint. I was helping a young man from Staten Island look for new jeans. He was gathering his denim, and I thought I stood to make a good commission, until he laid eyes on one of my coworkers. Sarah was a bubbly, blue-eyed blonde. A "pretty blonde."

It was like a switch flipped in his head. He ran up to her and started asking her opinion about the jeans he and I had already chosen, and at that point he completely tuned me out. Looking back, I was more bothered by his sudden rudeness than by potentially losing a decent sale. The fact that he thought it was okay to be rude and ignore me because this pretty blonde appeared sent a clear message.

Little by little, I started to understand what my coworker had meant. A pretty blonde would get picked up as a hitchhiker, and a pretty blonde could appear and result in me losing a sale. This was how things were set up, and it seemed I had to wake up and take notice. When I was working downtown around the trendy crowd, and as I explored new social scenes, I started noticing these dynamics more and more.

My consciousness of being brown was planted in elementary school. Being brown manifested in a real way through colorism among friendship cliques. I remember a group of girls who always sat and played together. They were all either mixed-race or light-skinned Black girls. There was only one brown-skinned girl in that group. She was an actress, and she had appeared in magazines. There is a tribalist quality about this that was hard for me not to notice. The shade or richness of your brown skin can determine where you fall in social dynamics. It wasn't until adulthood that I was seriously able to make these connections about colorism. I've always had friends of all shades, but I felt more of an immediate, unconscious preference for other brown-skinned people, which I now realize is because of how society colorgraded us.

So, in that respect, there might also be some of those tribalist tendencies within me. Being a brown-skinned woman is its own unique experience within the sphere of Blackness. Colorism is prevalent in society, and therefore, as a brown-skinned girl, your relation to whiteness and your worth might be determined by your socioeconomic class, or Eurocentric beauty standards such as an aquiline nose, physique, or hair texture. The most popular brown celebrities are the ones who basically look like white dipped in chocolate, just like the Black Barbie doll that we were all introduced to as girls growing up. When David Bowie talked about his wife Iman as being a "classic beauty," it seems clear he was commenting on those features that society views as "classic." Classic as in Shakespeare. Classic as in old. Classic as in pure.

This was a long way from my father's magazine cutouts and planet Africana that I had descended from. A very long way.

MisogyNIGHT

Misogynoir is a term created by Black feminist Moya Bailey to describe misogyny directed towards Black women. I became fully aware of misogynoir when I started enjoying New York City's nightlife. Even Serena Williams, with all her success and privilege, experiences the effects of such societal attitudes towards Black women, but this brand of misogynoir seems different. What I'm talking about rarely seems addressed directly, understood, or even discussed.

It's about Black female desirability and beauty as social capital, and the environments and situations where it comes into play and is most authentically perpetuated. My eyes began to open to this after a few of my close male friends started getting into the nightclub promotion industry to make fast money and build connections. It was interesting to hear the kinds of things that my promoter friends told me about the nightlife regulations: how much their image mattered, and how race came into play.

A lot of things became really clear to me, but not as quickly as they should have. I was still very much protected in a bubble of self-pride, and I was naïve and oblivious to a lot of the negativity. But then I watched a few of my African male friends transform into straight-up sellouts right before my very eyes. They had so much ego, bravado, and flashiness while being completely disconnected from their inner worth.

These dudes only mattered at night. Their identity as Black men didn't matter past the fact that it gave them an advantage over Black women or made them into a fetish for a lot of curious white girls. This is what they had to play up. I saw these superficial standards as a test of integrity for these boys. It proved to be a test that a lot of them failed.

My good friend Maurice went from having an affinity for Asian girls and Asian culture to exclusively dating white models. He modified his personality, his values, and even his friends to accommodate this new lifestyle in the club world. Maurice and I had been very tight. We were both West African and we developed a brother/sister bond. He began working with another West African promoter named Mitch. Mitch had been in the business longer and knew the ropes.

The two of them became very popular, started working at more exclusive venues, and had some of the most popping parties. Mitch, however, was losing himself. He developed a huge ego. He didn't really speak to me, and from what I gathered, he didn't really like me. Maurice told me that he didn't like me because I wasn't a model. Mitch solely dated models, the whitest ones you could imagine. He was a very charming dude and people liked him, so he was able to fill up tables easily. He liked to roll around the city with models during the day and even drove them to their castings. The club owners loved him.

One night, one of the club owners from one of the hottest clubs told Mitch that he was bringing too many Black girls to the party. He was only to invite Black girls if they were "essential." Essential meant a Black girl with an undeniable social status that they felt would put her on the same level with the white girls around. That meant she had to be extra striking and/

or signed to a top agency. The clients weren't paying all that money to be around Black girls, so if they were there, they had to count! He got paranoid and stopped inviting his core group of African models that he had known for years. By that time, I had started making other friends and fell back from the intensity of Maurice and Mitch's party drama. I actually went out to dance and let loose and not to stand around for someone else to get paid.

I had friends that had quit working in nightlife after similar situations. My friend Jason had been told something along the same lines as Mitch. He didn't really work at clubs with intense image guidelines. He was just responsible for bringing lots of people to the club. On a slow night, one of the managers of the club, who was also a Black man, told him that if he couldn't bring white girls, he had to bring more girls overall. He told Jason, "Four Black girls are equal to one white girl." Jason quit working there and never changed his crowd. He kept his parties the way he wanted, and it was a "take it or leave it" deal with him.

Maurice eventually stopped working with Mitch. Mitch developed a reputation as a big asshole. The only people that had anything nice to say about him were the white models he was clinging to for his image, club managers, and the owners he was serving, or the male models he wanted to be like. One day, it seems that everything came to a head. Mitch's ego and his alcoholism intertwined explosively! He beat up his girlfriend, a skinny redhead with very fair skin. The picture of her badly beaten face began to circulate. One of his professional rivals took advantage of this incident and brought this picture to all the nightclubs where Mitch was working. They all banned him.

He fell off big time and never truly recovered. He spent a couple of years in jail after that and was recently deported back to Africa. All that peacocking and high living and he hadn't bothered getting his papers straight. He was worried about the wrong things, and now he's back in Africa. I recently saw a picture of him on his wedding day. He looked mature and happy. His wife—a brown-skinned woman. A man that I knew for almost a decade, and that I had never seen even dating a Black girl, was now married to a Black woman in Africa. That shit blew my mind. But my hope is that Mitch is evolving away from all those things he didn't need, and that he has found what really matters.

In the world of nightlife, these men found there was easy money to be made with gorgeous girls on their arms. They were living "the life," but the truth is that a high roller club promoter's success has a lot to do with misogynoir. Black girls were like roaches in the club to some of these venue owners. For the promoters, their future working for these venues depended, and still does depend, heavily on whether or not they were willing to play the game and essentially sell themselves out. A lot of these dudes were Black. They would have their checks docked if their tables weren't full or delivering the type of look the managers wanted.

I remember calling Maurice a "coon" once, and he asked me what it meant. I explained he was buying into and willfully portraying the stereotype many white people have of people in his profession. And he simply agreed. That's how far in he was. He told me the nightlife didn't really like Black girls. In the beginning, I thought my friends were changing on their own. I didn't realize they were being instructed, programmed to this new way of thinking. They went out of their way to forge friendships with girls they would *never* have hung out with, all to keep a roof over their heads, food on the table, and the lights on while feeling important.

I met a lot of cool people and loved going out and having fun, exploring, and dancing with my friends at popular venues.

But it was frustrating to witness these sellouts around me and the politics behind their behavior. There were people that I'd seen around for years who wouldn't bother talking to me or saying hello. But they would eagerly start up a conversation with a friend of mine because she appeared whiter and more valuable. There was incessant phoniness everywhere and people switching from hot to cold at the drop of a hat. I saw a lot of Black men caught up in the life and walking around as if they were superior because of this perceived status change. A good friend of mine stopped speaking to me entirely after he went into the industry because I didn't fit the mold of his crew. My promoter friends who didn't try so hard to fit in and who took out more Black girls were less respected and got paid a lot less.

White girls are a valuable commodity for Black men in club promotion. I even heard one Black dude in the scene ask one of my promoter friends, "Why are you always with so many Black girls?" Like we were somehow devaluing him, when the truth was, he valued himself more than they were capable of understanding. He was able to feel comfortable with his home-girls without fear of being judged by this tragically superficial, fake, and overtly racist scene. I saw promoters who only used to roll in with Black girls do a complete 180 and dump their Black girlfriends to hang with much whiter crowds. Some of those bouncers were nightmares too! A few of them were extra whitewashed and seemed angrier than necessary. But that all trickled down from the attitude and views of the owners. The more racist the venue, the more entitled and disrespectful the bouncers. Maybe it was the pressure they felt, but it was apparent that they went out of their way to befriend white girls and were assholes to Black girls.

It was hard for me to get past witnessing a white man who was comfortable telling a Black man not to bring too many Black girls into a New York City venue that regularly hosted

Black celebrities. This was overt discrimination and complete disrespect. After that, a man pretty much belongs to the club and has lost himself. He might as well be the bottle of Svedka in the ice bucket, because he is allowing himself to be consumed by degenerates.

Out of the guys that I know who played the game, a few of them are still in the business. There are some who crashed and burned pretty hard after their fall and others just disappeared. A couple guys even died. Maurice quit promoting and disappeared.

I find it intriguing that, despite this misogynoir, all of these high roller venues cater almost entirely to ballers and bankers, and they rely heavily on them for their image. I always wonder how aware these celebrities are, and how these venues manage to pull the wool over their eyes so effectively. They are operating on a quota system, and they are playing music in the clubs that ninety percent of the people in there can't dance to. To be honest, I don't think any of these celebrities even care. They like to feel exclusive themselves and like the elite atmosphere it provides. At the end of the day, this is a deep systemic problem that is hard to change, even when it's obvious. Just know that if you hear something about racism and misogynoir in the nightlife scene in New York City, it's probably the truth.

My upbringing provided a shield from a lot of anti–Black girl attitudes. However, there are still a lot of people who need saving. A couple years ago, a popular rapper made some cringe-worthy statements about dark-skinned Black women. To me, it served as another reminder how prevalent this mentality is. Many people excuse this behavior as a man simply stating his preference.

Consider this: this so-called preference has made a lot of dark-skinned Black girls feel undateable and ugly. Ironically, I've sometimes felt more tokenized by Black men than by the white guys I've dated. I've had Black guys come right out and say, "I'm not usually attracted to Black girls, but I like you." Believe it or not, they consider this a compliment. They really think I should feel privileged for being on the receiving end of an attraction normally reserved for white girls.

Have they all gone mad? Nigga, ya mama's Black too. If they are alright with accepting their own sense of inferiority that's cool, but leave that shit over there. Clearly their melanin and my melanin aren't the same. Because I know that melanin exists across all seven kingdoms, and this African skin of mine will remain intact for years to come. So having more of it damn sure ain't make me less of anything. These people aren't thinking.

It's like these men are under a trance or in a deep sleep. They are victims of a coon control regiment, firmly enslaved in a mind-control bubble and floating merrily around in it, oblivious to the damage it's doing. Every time I've discussed this issue with girlfriends of mine, they always erupt in anger and agreement. This hits home for a lot of them. Feeling excluded by men that they share similar backgrounds with. Being sold out for social acceptance. For some, being told they weren't as pretty in their adolescence only to be reminded and triggered back to that age and those experiences. Drastically being reduced, erased, or eliminated. The only sane thing to do is to avoid these spaces and these people to spare your mental health.

I had developed friendships with some of these guys over time, and it was interesting to witness how much they chased an image. They had become so disconnected from Black women and had placed so much value upon white womanhood while stripping it from themselves.

Through it all, I saw the mental toll that this intense level of whitewashing can take on the psyche. It makes people mean and it's divisive as hell. Misogynoir and colorism are pervasive problems for the Black community. We need to take back, and rejoice in, our Blackness.

I believe that we should all become more like the abolitionists and again take on the task of freeing the slaves rather than persecuting them. I have felt a lot of pity for Black men and women who share that misogynoir mentality. And I simply wish that everyone had the opportunity to grow up with the same kinds of enriching, restorative images and affirmations of Blackness I did. I have no doubt that this made all the difference in how I see and value myself. I firmly believe this is the most powerful way to control this issue. It starts before any real assimilation is made outside the home. But along with that, misogynoir needs to be confronted and addressed head-on. Black women are bearing the heaviest burden by far. Enough!

360° Womanhood

*You know when girls say,
"I'm a girl's girl?" It has never felt
right for me to say that because
I don't know if I'm a girl's girl.
I think I might be
a full woman's woman.*
—Charlize Theron

A tarot card reader once told me that there are people who feel threatened by my independence. I took this to refer to other women feeling threatened. A couple of other readers have told me that I would fare better with male friendships. One even summed it up quite directly: "Women are not your friends." I never took this too much to heart or let it make me especially cautious or distrusting of other women. I realized that acting from this point of view would add to the problem and would in fact be subscribing to a degree of self-hatred. I am well aware of constructs that shape competition between women. It's bigger than just pointing the finger at women. But my awareness didn't mean that I didn't put any stock in it either. I have to admit that these observations made a lot of sense when looking back at my life and the situations I've faced.

Maybe the insight of the tarot readers was referring specifically to my friendships with women who display animosity and passive-aggressive behavior? In friendships, I have felt put down even though I wasn't signaling any hostility or need to compete. Because I always just do me. And sometimes that works out for me. But this is perplexing to people who don't understand my choices, people who never expected me to succeed. My success might seem like a threat to women who are struggling to play by the rules. Men, on the other hand, don't initially view me as a threat because they are coming from a place of privilege and therefore my relative success doesn't bother them.

Independence is a very peculiar thing for someone to feel threatened by. It doesn't seem like something that people should covet. It's not fame, beauty, status, or wealth. Independence is autonomy. But the psychic's statement seemed particularly relevant because I consider my independence a definitive part of me. Aside from my thoughtfulness and my ability to write, independence is all I have. At the root of it all is a decision to indulge in the faith I have in myself. I trust me. I trust myself as a vessel of purpose and I'm hoping that the shit pays off. As someone with an artistic streak, being independent involves being enslaved to a domineering creative spirit. I've found that this only ever becomes a point of contention or envy for others when it starts paying off. When that happens, people look at you and think how incredible it is that you have succeeded in living the unorthodox life that you chose.

But when it isn't working, you are seen as a loser in many people's eyes. When others can't figure out what you're doing and it's not making sense to them, they will definitely let you know. A couple years ago, I met up with a friend that I hadn't seen in a while. We had fallen out in the past and were working on mending things. We were giving each other updates on our lives. He was doing well for himself and was telling me about all the properties he was looking to purchase. He has always been very driven and hardworking, so I expected him to succeed. He was also a very catty type of dude. At that point in life, I was still figuring out my creative direction; I definitely wasn't thinking about real estate. In the midst of his boastfulness, he turned to me, shrugged, and asked, quite casually, "Why don't you just get married?" It was probably one of the most fucked up things anyone has ever said to me. He might as well have shanked me with a shard.

I knew what he meant by it. This was his way of communicating to me that he thought I was a failure, and that my only way out would be through a wealthy man's rescue. But I also believed that deep down, he was afraid of me. He was afraid of my independence and the possibility that my creativity would take me to a place that would outshine him. This is what all women are up against. We are expected to be chosen by a man to ensure our security, and not expected to achieve our own success. But I wasn't looking to be chosen.

A few years after that, when I started to develop my direction and the winning seemed to be kicking in, another friend displayed a passive-aggressive attitude towards me. It didn't seem quite as extreme as jealousy, but it was definitely a sense of frustration. She once blurted out, "You can just do whatever you want and people like it." Of course, this was not true. The people who connect to my point of view express it, and those that don't also express it. This creates a conversation, and that's what makes it matter. I wanted to tell her that my way was the hard way of doing things. If she wanted to do things this way too, she could. But it would mean taking a lot more risks, and trading in any sense of security from this world.

On my journey, I discovered that there's a lot more internal work to just doing me. My sense of independence and liberation is not just about being strong in front of a man. It has a lot to do with understanding the influence of the patriarchy on me regarding my relationships with other women. My liberation involves recognizing and actively working to change this. I must engage in self-evaluation. How does my own insecurity apply? Am I jealous of other women? Do I want the women around me to thrive? Am I happy with them thriving? Am I *helping* them thrive? That's freedom. Can I stand beside a woman that I consider more beautiful, talented, intelligent, creative, and magnetic than I am, and help her thrive? Even if that may mean her outshining me and winning? Can I do that because I understand that a win for another woman in the grand scheme is one for us all? Am I comfortable enough within my own skin to withstand this? Woman to woman, feminist to womanist? Friend to friend? Boss bitch to boss bitch? Sister to sister?

Not just walking alongside another powerful woman but possibly even pulling her up from the trenches, making those introductions for her, and letting her be great. Nothing beats that—that's freedom. Knowing how I as a woman can help out another *and doing it,* selflessly. That's what I call a woman's woman and the only type of woman I want as a friend. Women like that will always make shit happen. When you become that woman, you will attract more of those women.

This is an act of protest and defiance. It's a statement—I am not meant to just be chosen. I am a provider as well. I don't accept any compliment that comes from putting another woman down. I am not motivated by the need to outshine other women.

I'm motivated to build entire networks of us.

What the psychic should have said was that the problem isn't women. It's how the patriarchy handles a woman who isn't seeking to compete and just wants to live the life she chooses. How the world doesn't necessarily want women to have this formula for winning. How doing you in a bold way is a quality that can be magnetic to some while stirring up a real sense of insecurity in others.

So, what can this mean through a feminist lens? It means seeking completion on your own terms, whatever that may mean to you. 360° womanhood and the rejection of toxic masculinity for something more like divine masculinity. It means being independent of the bullshit while doing the most for others.

Burnt Out

You can't just come in when people have a culture that's been laid down for generations and you come in and now shit gotta change because you're here? Get the fuck outta here. Can't do that!
—Spike Lee

Gentrification is a system structured with the primary goal of increasing and attracting white middle class and affluent residents into the hood communities. I lived in pre-gentrified Harlem with my mom after my parents split. Long before a fucking Whole Foods was built there, before the bougie-ass coffee house negroes showed up, and ages before what my friends and I dubbed "Caucasian Sundays" were a regular thing. Pregentrified Harlem is what I know, and as a native New Yorker,

the current changes take some getting used to. If you're a person of color and have lived in the hood, chances are you have a gentrification story. Chances are you think it's bullshit.

Our apartment building burned down on Thanksgiving weekend when I was in my mid-teens. We were living on Morningside Avenue, just a few blocks away from the Apollo Theater and facing Morningside Park. It was a pretty spacious apartment with four bedrooms and one and a half bathrooms. The rent was $800 a month.

I didn't know it when I lived there, but the building was really old. After it burned down, it made the front page of the paper. We discovered that one of our neighbors was over one hundred years old, and had been living there since before the civil rights movement. I was horrified to realize how much history had been erased with the burning of the building.

The night of the fire, I escaped with my pajama pants, my black Gap coat, my gray Jordans, and nothing else. The entire building was evacuated, and we all stood in the park as the firefighters tried to put out the flames. Because our apartment faced the street, I had a clear view of my mother's bedroom engulfed in flames. I screamed for hours until my voice gave out. Thank God nobody from the building died that day. We did, however, lose two of our neighbors to the emotional despair and shock of being left homeless in the wintertime. Two of the African fathers from the building died within a month of the fire.

Afterwards, we all worked on getting our lives together and finding new places to live. Most of us were scattered throughout the city's shelter system. The landlord secretly contacted all the families and gave us each a check to help get ourselves together. My mother and I got $5,000, and our neighbors from downstairs, the family of one of the deceased African fathers, received a little less.

Every family from that night was accounted for except one, which was peculiar. According to the report, the building burned down because one of our neighbors was smoking weed and passed out, then the fire took over. That story always seemed suspect as hell to me, because nobody from the building ever saw this woman again! Not even on the night of the fire. Speculation began to grow that this story was bullshit, and that she had somehow been part of a scheme orchestrated by the landlord to burn us out. We all left the building the night of the fire believing that one day we would return. But what we didn't realize was that an era of Harlem had burned down along with our building. That building would no longer be ours. Period. Harlem itself was no longer for any of us.

Years later, they rebuilt that building, complete with marble floors and $8,000-per-month duplex apartments. It is now inhabited by gentrifiers and affluent hipster transplants. With its doorman and predominantly white tenants, it seems to be completely devoid of people with any neighborhood history to contribute to future generations. To add insult to injury, our neighbor from the building next to ours, which didn't burn at all, managed to use our story and profit off of our tragedy. He called the TV show *Maury* and got his daughter, a girl no older than eleven, to lie about being one of the families from the fire. The footage they aired on the show was of my mother's room in flames. My mother and I sat and watched the show while we were still displaced and living in the shelter system. It was devastating. Maury Povich, the host, gave the family a brand-new apartment on Morningside Drive, along with a laptop for the little girl and a bunch of cool swag. These people were frauds, and the people from my building had to see this all on the *Maury* show.

I recall feeling extremely isolated during that period. I had become confused and disillusioned with life. I took long walks through Harlem in the wintertime and listened to music to decompress before having to return to the shelter. But I returned to school after the fire as if nothing had happened. I remember not wanting my friends or really anyone to know the details or the extent of how lost and destitute I was. I didn't need people gasping in my face and inundating me with useless pity. I suppose I also didn't know how to receive support and had done my best to avoid emotion. At that time, I knew how to think about things, but didn't allow myself to feel things.

An English teacher that I got along very well with gave me some of his wife's old clothes, which I accepted. None of my classmates offered me anything, but I was cool with that. They thought I was okay. I was really good at being okay when I was not okay. But these were some fucked up circumstances and I don't know how to ever be okay with that. Maybe if it had been an accidental fire, I would have been more okay. But knowing that our landlord was willing to risk our lives for some insurance money and to lure in gentrifiers they could overcharge? What the fuck?! I could have died that cold November.

I later learned that there was nothing new at all about this system of landlords burning down buildings for insurance, only to flip them years later for more money. As landlords are learning that their properties' value can skyrocket, they are resorting to extreme measures to get longtime residents out. There has been a surge in these types of dangerous sabotages. It's illegal, unethical, and currently a serious problem in North Brooklyn. Yet very few people seem to be paying attention to the details and truth of this practice.

So no, I'm not okay with any of the shit I see going on in Manhattan and Brooklyn and I don't give a fuck how anyone feels about it. It's not as simple as a white person just moving into a neighborhood. There's an entire ruthless system in place that goes to great lengths so folks can idly move in and be oblivious to what's going on around them. They have the privilege of rolling their eyes or getting defensive whenever the topic of gentrification is brought up. It's ignorance and indifference. I hope people will start to pay attention more and some sort of system of alert and protection for buildings that are at risk can be created. These gentrifiers should be just as burdened moving into these neighborhoods as the families that have been living there for generations are now!

It's been years since that fire, but ultimately I kept it burning inside.